The Care and Display of the
American Flag

The Care and Display of the
American Flag

BY THE EDITORS OF SHARPMAN.COM®

Stewart, Tabori & Chang

New York

Illustrations by Laura D'Argo

Published in 2004 by
Stewart, Tabori & Chang
A Company of La Martinière Groupe
115 West 18th Street
New York, NY 10011

Canadian Distribution:
Canadian Manda Group
One Atlantic Avenue, Suite 105
Toronto, Ontario M6K 3E7
Canada

Library of Congress Cataloging-in-Publication Data

The care and display of the American flag / by the editors of SharpMan.com.
        p. cm
   Includes bibliographical references and index.
   ISBN: 1-58479-321-X
     1. Flags—United States. I. SharpMan.com.

  CR113.C37 2004
     929.9'2—dc22   2003067275

Edited by Jennifer Lang
Designed by Galen Smith and Kristine Platou
Graphic Production by Kim Tyner

Printed in Singapore

10 9 8 7 6 5 4 3 2 1

First Printing

Front Cover: World War II-era, 48-star American flag

The text of this book was composed in Meridien and Franklin Gothic

This is dedicated to the Boy and Girl Scouts of America,
the civil and military personnel who serve our country, and all
Americans who proudly fly our flag.

Contents

Introduction

"THE THINGS THAT THE FLAG STANDS FOR were created by the experiences of a great people. Everything that it stands for was written by their lives. The flag is the embodiment, not of sentiment, but of history."

Woodrow Wilson, June 14, 1915, Flag Day

The flag of the United States is more than a piece of cloth. As President Woodrow Wilson said almost a century ago, it is the embodiment of the people and the history of the United States. It is imbued with the blood and sacrifice of those who went before us, but also with the hopes and dreams of all who have come to this land to experience the opportunities of freedom. Whether they were tired and hungry, persecuted and harassed, or just wanted their children to have a better chance at happiness, the life of every person who has ever come to America is sewn into the American flag.

Before 1777, when the first official United States flag was created through a resolution of the Continental Congress, national flags were the property of monarchs and dictators. They symbolized not the will of the people but the power of the crown. In Great Britain, even after the American Revolution, the average citizen was not allowed to fly a flag. The Union Jack, the official flag of the United Kingdom, was reserved specifically for property owned by the king. Merchant ships and others with permission to fly a national flag were given a special, lesser banner to fly.

These traditions are still alive in many countries today. In Peru, there are two official flags, one for the government and one for citizens. In England, the flag is almost always used as a symbol of antigovernment sentiment, not patriotism. In India, citizens were only recently given the right to own and fly the national flag.

For the first one hundred years of our history, very few Americans flew the national flag. It was not until the Civil War, when the flag and the very union it stood for came under fire, that the flag became a public symbol. In 1887, contemporary flag historian George Henry Preble wrote, "Every city, town and village suddenly blossomed with banners. On forts and ships, from church spires and flag staffs, from colleges, hotel buildings, store fronts, and private balconies, from public edifices, everywhere the old flag was flung out, and everywhere it was hailed with enthusiasm." The American love affair with the flag has not ceased since.

From the day it was created, the American flag has been for and about the American people. From day one you, the average American, have had the right and the privilege to fly the Stars and Stripes. As citizens, we take this right for granted, but it was a revolution in the history of national symbols. The flag is not *theirs*—whether this refers to the government, a corporation, or a ruling class— it is *ours*.

"THE FLAG REPRESENTS a living country and is itself considered a living thing."

U.S. Code, Title 4, Chapter 1, Section 8(j)

With the right to fly the United States flag, however, comes the responsibility to fly it properly. In past years, many Americans can likely recall seeing torn and faded flags hanging awkwardly from wires across public streets. They may have also seen flags hanging out of windows at night, covered with bird droppings, or a flag flying from the overpass of a highway that was so ripped and torn that it was barely recognizable as the Stars and Stripes. In my neighborhood, not ten blocks from my house, a man mounted an American flag directly above his chimney. Then he went inside and lit a fire! In a matter of weeks, the flag was blackened and begrimed almost beyond recognition, and yet almost a year later it still flies there, like an old forgotten dishrag in a dirty kitchen sink.

Flying the flag is a patriotic act, and we all applaud those whose pride of country compels them to show their solidarity with the American ideals we all cherish. If you are reading this book, you are probably one of the millions of proud owners of an American flag. May your banner always wave free and represent the best of what is in your heart and mind.

Always remember that the flag you possess is a "living" thing. The statute quoted on the previous page does not say the flag is to be "treated" like a living thing; it says the flag is to be "considered" a living thing. Like any living thing, you must nurture it, and always treat it with respect.

Flying the American flag—any flag, of any size, in any condition—shows public spirit, but leaving it out overnight in inclement weather, allowing it to get entangled on its staff or in a nearby tree, or standing by as it becomes soiled and ragged, is lazy and foolish. Would you stand idly by as your pet or a child became filthy and injured? And yet many would allow their flags to fall into a similar state of decay. This is clearly the kind of halfhearted patriotism that does not do the flag owner or this country proud.

What about lesser errors in flag display and care, however, such as hanging a flag backward or in the wrong place? Flag etiquette can be surprisingly complex, and yet it forms the basis for being an active, alert, and patriotic American citizen. That is why the editors of SharpMan.com have created this helpful guide, because when you know the rules and are willing to follow them, you are doing a service to yourself, to your community, and to the country of which you are a part.

Bret Witter
editor-at-large, SharpMan.com

The United States Flag Code

In the first 150 years of our country's history, there were no national rules regarding the care and display of the American flag. Every group that wanted to fly the flag simply created its own procedures, which often varied widely. At one point the U.S. Army observed completely different regulations than did the U.S. Navy, which didn't have much in common with the rules followed by the Coast Guard. This was unfortunate but not deadly—until the tanks started rolling in 1917 and the soldiers headed for the trenches in Europe. Witnessing the horrors of World War I resulted in this country deciding on a new way of thinking about a lot of things, and one of those things was the purpose of the American flag.

On June 14, 1923, representatives of the army, navy, and sixty-six other national organizations finally met to hammer out common ground rules on the care and display of the American flag. Calling themselves the National Flag Conference, this group developed and adopted a National Flag Code that prescribed the correct way to fly and respect the flag. The group met again on Flag Day in 1924 to modify the code. Representatives of all sixty-eight groups took the new code back to their members, and from that day forward . . . nothing happened.

It was not until June 22, 1942, while the war that had started in Europe was exploding into American living rooms and American lives, that Congress passed a joint resolution calling for the passage of the National Flag Code into United States law. And with good reason. Six months earlier, flag sales exploded in the wake of the attack on Pearl Harbor, and with patriotism running at an all-time high, the government sought a way to mold that fervor into a positive, unified front. What better way than to give every American an agreed-upon, federally-backed manner of displaying their flags, the ultimate symbol of American pride and strength?

On December 22, 1942, just slightly more than a year after the bombing of Pearl Harbor, the National Flag Code became Public Law 829, Chapter 806, Seventy-seventh Congress, Second Session. A month later, it was officially written into the United States Code.

UNITED STATES CODE, TITLE 4, CHAPTER 1

The United States Code is the official compilation of the permanent laws of the United States currently in force. It is administered by the Office of the Law Revision Council of the United States House of Representatives and officially updated every January. This body is given the power to compile the code by— what else?—the U.S. Code itself, in Title 2, Section 285(b).

The United States Code is broken down into fifty areas by subject matter. Each subject consists of titles, chapters, sections, subtitles, subchapters, parts, subparts, and divisions. Fifty areas doesn't sound like much, does it? Well, it is. The code comprises more than eight hundred chapters and eighty thousand sections. It is more than ten thousand standard pages long, and it continues to grow every year.

The part of the code that addresses the care and display of the American flag is Title 4 (Flag and Seal, Seat of Government, and the States), Chapter 1, Sections 1–10. Downloaded from the Internet, it's fifteen pages long, a mere drop in the governmental bucket. These fifteen pages are meant for civilian (nonmilitary) citizens of the United States. Further rules for military and wartime usage of the flag are found in Title 36 (Patriotic Societies and Observations). The code does not allow any federal agency to issue "official" rulings regarding the flag or to change the flag regulations in any way. Only the president of the United States is empowered to amend, delete, or create additional rules.

Some penalties for abuse of the flag are found in Title 18 (Crimes and Criminal Procedure). However, for the most part, the code does not impose penalties for misuse or abuse of the American flag. If you drag a flag through the mud, wear it as a sweater, or forget to haul it to the top of the flagpole before lowering it to half-staff, you are violating the United States Code but you're not going to serve any prison time. The right to fine, incarcerate, or otherwise penalize a citizen for disrespect is left to each state, and most don't strictly enforce these rules and regulations. Of course, this doesn't mean we shouldn't know and respect the laws of the land. If you are proud enough of your country to fly its flag, you should care enough to follow its laws—even if the authorities are looking the other way.

How to Use This Book

This book provides a complete record of the official *federal* rules regarding the American flag, as well as all the unofficial accepted traditions commonly associated with proper flag care. Do you have a question regarding a particular flag-related situation? The answer is in this book, usually with its own dedicated section. Look up the situation in the table of contents and turn to the appropriate page. It's that simple.

Within each section you will find:

THE CODE An excerpt from the United States Code or other government regulation with an easy-to-understand reference to where it is found in the code, rather than a legal citation;

IN OTHER WORDS An explanation of the legal language;

FOR EXAMPLE An example of how the U.S. Code applies to real-world experiences and situations;

ALSO Additional conventions based on the code, when applicable;

WHY IS THIS? An explanation of why the rule is part of the flag's tradition. This includes any accepted conventions that have grown out of a code clause. For instance, there is nothing in the flag code regarding the proper folding of the American flag. However, the tradition of folding the flag thirteen times is an important aspect of caring for the American flag;

DID YOU KNOW? The history of the law, including any significant persons or events associated with its passage, use, or abuse.

Since laws and penalties differ by state, this book features the basic laws and penalties for the District of Columbia as a proxy for generally applied regulations. The District of Columbia is under the direct jurisdiction of the federal government, and therefore its laws regarding the American flag are contained in the United States Code. When this section of the code is cited, a notation will explain, for example, that any penalties apply to the District of Columbia only. For further information on your local laws and regulations, check with your state government.

PART ONE

The History and Meaning of the American Flag

The Creation of a National Symbol

RESOLVED THAT THE FLAG OF THE UNITED STATES be made of thirteen stripes, alternate red and white; that the union be thirteen stars, white in a blue field, representing a new constellation.

Marine Committee of the Continental Congress, June 14, 1777

IN OTHER WORDS

The flag of the United States was created with one rather imprecise sentence, and with no fanfare, by a subcommittee of the Continental Congress almost a year after the Declaration of Independence—an inauspicious beginning for one of the most recognized emblems in the world.

FOR EXAMPLE

The flag must have thirteen stripes and thirteen stars, but notice that there is nothing in this resolution that specifies the direction of the stripes or the arrangement of the stars, among other considerations.

WHY IS THIS?

The subcommittee was likely vague about the actual design of the American flag because there was already a flag in use. It is now called the Continental Colors, and it was flown for the first time at the Battle of Bunker Hill in Boston. The Continental Colors featured the thirteen red and white stripes but had a small

British flag in the upper left corner instead of the blue field and stars. This caused confusion: Were the Americans fighting for a new country or just for more rights within the British empire? A circle of stars replaced the small version of the British flag to clear up this confusion, and thus they are referred to as "a new constellation," signifying an entirely new country.

But why was this a matter for a marine subcommittee charged with overseeing waterborne commerce? The answer has to do with the law of the sea. Even today, as during the Revolutionary War, a ship cannot dock unless it sails under the flag of a sovereign nation. American ships were no longer flying the British Union Jack and lacked their own flag, prompting American merchants to pressure Congress into action.

The Continental Colors flag, flown by American Revolutionary fighters.

DID YOU KNOW?

The resolution creating the American flag was sandwiched between a resolution on protecting the Delaware River in case of a British attack and a discussion of whether one Captain Roach should be replaced as the commander of the continental warship *Ranger*. Congress gave itself control of warships in the Delaware, the general design of the flag was set, and, a minute later, Captain Roach was replaced in his command by John Paul Jones, the man known today as the father of the American navy.

The Design of the First American Flag

No one knows who designed the Continental Colors, one of many flags carried by American forces at the first official battle of the Revolutionary War. The stripes were the symbol of the Sons of Liberty, the most ardent early fighters for American patriotism, but as to which son (or daughter) designed the stripes, it is not known. We do know, however, who designed the first official American flag, the one that has served as the basis for all of our nation's subsequent flags.

Betsy Ross, right? Well, actually, no.

Most historians believe that the American flag was designed by Francis Hopkinson, a signer of the Declaration of Independence, member of the Marine

Committee from New Jersey, and an acknowledged seal and symbol enthusiast. Hopkinson took the stripes from the Continental Colors and combined them with a "new constellation" of stars— thirteen in a circle to represent the equality of the thirteen colonies—on a field of blue to symbolize the new country. It is likely he presented the design to the Marine Committee for their approval before they passed the flag res-

The first American flag, 1777.

olution. In other words, the delegates were simply agreeing to and describing the design Hopkinson had already created.

Betsy Ross sewed the first flag, though, right? Alas, probably not.

The legend of Betsy Ross and the American flag dates back to 1870, almost a hundred years after the creation of the first flag, when her grandson William Canby gave a speech to the Pennsylvania Historical Society and made the claim that his grandmother created the first American flag. In Canby's version of events, George Washington and two others came to Betsy Ross's house in the spring of 1776 with a rough sketch of the flag, which she modified and sewed. In fact, this meeting probably never took place and, even if it did, the first American flag was not created until more than a year later. It is true that Betsy Ross sewed flags, and sewed them very well, but it is disputed by many that she had anything to do with the design or creation of the Stars and Stripes.

Even so, Betsy Ross is a national hero and one of the most famous people in the early history of the United States. In fact, if you buy a replica of the first American flag, the one with thirteen stripes and thirteen stars in a circle, it is known officially as the Betsy Ross flag.

Meanwhile, Francis Hopkinson has been largely forgotten. His design is one of the most well-known images in history, but his personal fame has long since been eclipsed. However, modern Americans aren't the only ones to blame for this. Even in his day, Hopkinson's achievement was underappreciated. No one disputed that he designed the flag, but then again, no one wanted to pay him for his work either. In later years, when Hopkinson attempted to get reimbursed for his expenses in creating the flag, Congress repeatedly quibbled with him over his paperwork and receipts. After being told numerous times, essentially, "I'm sorry, sir, you'll have to fill out this paperwork, and this new form, and have that notarized, and then come back tomorrow," Hopkinson gave up.

What was the exorbitant price Hopkinson wanted to be paid for designing our national emblem? Why, little more than a "quarter cask of the public wine" in recognition of his services. A cask of wine he never received.

Ah, bureaucracy!

The Stripes

IN OTHER WORDS

The U.S. Code leaves a lot to the imagination when it comes to the stripes on the American flag. The first is the width of the stripes, which by convention are all the same. The second is which color stripe should come first. While early flags often differed, it soon became accepted practice for the red stripe to appear on the outside (top and bottom) of the flag. A popular theory explains that this is because white stripes get dirty faster. The real reason is probably because the flag looks better with the red stripes on the outside.

FOR EXAMPLE

Before the number and color of stripes were set, American flags varied widely. Most featured thirteen stripes and a blue field of stars, but the stripes were often red, white, and blue—the favorite color pattern of Benjamin Franklin. Several well-known early flags even had vertical stripes. The famed Bennington flag, which has the number 76 written in the union, had white stripes on the outside.

The design of the stripes was codified on November 27, 1981, in the General Service Administration "Federal Specification, Flag, National, United States of America and the Flag Union Jack," DDD-F-416E. This code, reactivated in December 2002, stipulates the exact design and construction specifications for every American flag, including details such as acceptable material (cotton, nylon, and rayon) and acceptable stitching styles for more than a dozen different elements. The thirty-four-page-long text states: "The flag shall consist of 13 horizontal stripes, 7 red and 6 white, which shall alternate beginning and ending with red stripe."

WHY IS THIS?

The thirteen stripes stand for the thirteen original colonies, featured equally.

DID YOU KNOW?

Even after the Continental Congress resolution of 1777, the thirteen red and white stripes were not fixed. The problem came with the admittance of Vermont and Kentucky as the fourteenth and fifteenth states. On January 13, 1794, Congress passed a resolution creating a flag with fifteen stars and fifteen stripes to accommodate these new states. It soon became clear, however, that adding stripes for states wasn't going to work. After all, fifty stripes—or even thirty stripes—are visually problematic. In 1818, Congress passed a resolution stabilizing the number of stripes at the original thirteen.

The Bennington flag.

The Stars

IN OTHER WORDS

The stars are the most complicated element of the flag. Since there are so many of them, the arrangement must be precisely defined. Most people think of the rows and columns when they think of the flag, but the fact that the stars form neat diagonals, and that all stars are five-pointed with one point straight up, is actually what gives the field of stars its orderly appearance.

FOR EXAMPLE

Before the creation of the American flag, the five-pointed star was extremely rare. In fact, very few flags even had stars on them. When they did, most used either a six-pointed star (George Washington's favorite) or a starburst—a circle with many small arms that imitate the way actual stars look to the human eye.

Because of its inclusion on the American flag, the five-pointed star is now the most common type of star shape in the world.

WHY IS THIS?

The five-pointed star was adopted for convenience. Early American flags were all hand-cut and -sewn and being able to create stars quickly was vital to meeting the huge demand for the new flags. Unlike six-pointers and starbursts, which are difficult to cut, a five-pointed star can be made with one cut.

DID YOU KNOW?

The most enduring part of the Betsy Ross legend is that she suggested the five-pointed star and showed George Washington how it could easily be cut. While the George Washington part of the story is probably untrue, it is likely true that a Philadelphia seamstress did suggest the five-pointed star. Whether this seamstress was Betsy Ross is unknown.

The Number of Stars

IN OTHER WORDS

Every time a state is added to the union, the flag "grows" by one star. Since 1818, the stars have been the only element of the American flag to change.

FOR EXAMPLE

The U.S. Code, created in 1942, states that "the union of the flag shall be forty-eight stars, white in a blue field." This reflects the fact that Alaska and Hawaii did not become states until 1959.

ALSO

The fiftieth star, for Hawaii, was added by Dwight Eisenhower's Executive Order No. 10834, published August 25, 1959. On the Fourth of July, 1960, along with the new star for Alaska, Hawaii's star changed the old forty-eight-star flag to the American flag we know today.

WHY IS THIS?

The stars represent the states, and therefore each new state means the addition of a new star. Because the pattern of the stars is so precise, each new star also means that the arrangement of the stars must be completely redesigned.

So who designed the current pattern of stars? The answer is . . . an Ohio high school student named Robert Heft, who spent twelve and a half hours one weekend sewing a new arrangement of stars for a class project in 1949. He got a B minus, but his teacher promised to raise his grade if he could get Congress to accept the design. Heft sent the flag to his local congressman and to his utter amazement—and no doubt the amazement of his tough-grading teacher—it became the official flag of the United States.

DID YOU KNOW?

The current fifty-star flag design has lasted longer than any other flag design in United States history. Why? Because this is by far the longest period in the nation's history without the addition of a new state. But don't worry, if a fifty-first state is ever added, Robert Heft has already designed a fifty-one-star flag.

The Colors of the Flag

THE COLORS OF THE U.S. NATIONAL FLAG ARE AS FOLLOWS:

Old Glory Red   Cable No. 70180
White   Cable No. 70001
Old Glory Blue   Cable No. 70075

General Services Administration (GSA) "Federal Specification, Flag,
National, United States of America and Flag, Union Jack," DDD-F-416E, Clause 3.4

IN OTHER WORDS

It's not just red, white, and blue up there on that emblem, those are very specific shades of red, white, and blue. The white and the blue are common colors, but the red in the flag is a very uncommon shade. In fact, it is not produced for any purpose other than the American flag.

FOR EXAMPLE

Without specific color references, the flag could vary immensely. It could even be aqua, cream, and pink—that is, if someone wanted to argue that those colors were actually "red, white, and blue" as stated in the U.S. Code.

ALSO

Charles Thomson, secretary of Congress, 1782, described the newly designed Great Seal of the United States (both sides of which, one bearing the eagle and the other a pyramid, are found on the back of the dollar bill) this way: "The colours of the pales are those used in the flag of the United States of America; White signifies purity and innocence, Red, hardiness and valour, and Blue, the colour of the Chief, signifies vigilance, perseverance, and justice."

WHY IS THIS?

The Great Seal of the United States used the colors of the flag, since these were now the colors of the country, but Charles Thomson's description was the first time anyone ascribed any meaning to the colors. Did Thomson make up the meanings of the colors we use on our flag? Probably not. The Founding Fathers simply adopted the colors for the United States flag from the British flag.

DID YOU KNOW?

It was possible to easily make only eight types of dye in colonial America: light blue, indigo (dark blue), red, white, yellow, gold, black, and green. Yellow is the color of quarantine, so it was used on very few official flags at the time. Black has always been the color of death in western culture, not the best choice for an eternal beacon of freedom and justice. That leaves just green, gold, and light blue as the colors not chosen by Francis Hopkinson for use in his flag design.

Old Glory

After the "Stars and Stripes," "Old Glory" is probably today's most popular nickname for the American flag. Yet few realize that, in the beginning, Old Glory didn't refer to all American flags, but to only one American flag—the treasured possession of a sea captain named William Driver.

In 1831, Captain Driver was commissioned to sail from his home in Salem, Massachusetts, on the brig *Charles Doggett*—a voyage that would culminate with the rescue of the mutineers from the HMS *Bounty*. As he prepared to sail, some friends presented him with a beautifully crafted American flag. When the flag unfurled from the masthead for the first time, Captain Driver exclaimed, "Old Glory!"

The term didn't catch on until more than thirty years later, however, during the Civil War, when Union troops marched on the state of Tennessee. By this time, Captain Driver had long since retired to Nashville, Tennessee. His personal flag was the most famous Stars and Stripes in the city, so when the state seceded from the Union in 1861, Confederate troops planned to drive home the point with a public burning of Old Glory. Try as they might, though, they couldn't find the flag.

When Union troops captured Nashville in 1862, they immediately raised the American flag over the capitol building. The flag was warmly received, but . . . the emblem was small, a little battered, and, well, there was just something missing. People began to wonder, did Captain Driver still have Old Glory?

A delegation of Union troops went to Driver's house, where they followed the sixty-year-old sea captain into his bedroom and watched him tear open his quilt. Inside, hidden between the layers, was his beloved Old Glory. In order to keep the flag safe from Confederate troops, Captain Driver had sewn the flag into his bedspread, which he slept with across his chest every night. Old Glory was removed from its hiding place and, with great fanfare, hoisted over the capitol that very day.

The Sixth Ohio Regiment, a member of which had visited Captain Driver and had seen the flag hidden in the bedspread, was so enchanted by the story of Old Glory that the unit actually took the nickname for itself. The members also spread the story far and wide, telling and retelling it, until the name of the captain's cherished flag became synonymous with all American flags.

Old Glory still exists, but it is no longer available for public viewing.

The Proportions of the Flag

THE FOLLOWING SIZES OF FLAGS are authorized for executive agencies:

PROPORTIONS OF FLAG

Hoist (Width)	Fly (Length)
Feet	Feet
20.0	38.0
10.0	19.0
8.95	17.0
7.0	11.0
5.0	9.50
4.33	5.50
3.50	6.65

Executive Order No. 10834, issued by Dwight D. Eisenhower, August 21, 1959

IN OTHER WORDS

The official proportions call for the flag to be almost twice as long as it is wide. But is this what most flags look like? The answer is no, and it's not an optical illusion. Most flags are more square in shape, usually either 2:3 or 3:5. This is acceptable if the flag measurement is approved by a government inspector, because President Eisenhower's Executive Order (which follows proportions set forth by President Taft in 1912) only applies to flags flown for a limited number of official government uses.

FOR EXAMPLE

Flags come in all sizes. A 2:3 proportion simply means the measurements conform to this ratio. A 2:3 flag could be 4 inches by 6 inches (because if you divide by two you get 2:3), 8 feet by 12 feet (divide by four), 3 yards by 4.5 yards (divide by 1.5), or any other like measurement.

WHY IS THIS?

The evolution of modern flag proportions began in 1687 with an order from the British secretary of the Admiralty Samuel Pepys (yes, he also kept a famous diary). Pepys declared that all British naval flags would be one half yard long for every half breadth of *bewper* (a type of bunting fabric) used in their construction. The bewper of the day came in 22-inch-wide strips, so the proportions of the flags became 11 by 18 (18 inches being half a yard). In the 1770s, when the United States flag was created, bewper was only available in 19-inch wide strips, so the proportion of British flags was 9.5:18, very close to the 10:19 proportion used. More than a century and a half later, this ratio was adopted as the official proportion for the American flag. Confused? Don't be. Just use the simple 2:3 ratio. For information on decorating with today's bunting, see page 109.

The 10:19 measurement was first officially set forth in naval regulations dating back to 1862. The army, however, used a 10:18 proportion. In 1912, President Taft sided with the navy, requiring the army to change its flag by Executive Order. These proportions remain the official proportions of the current flag.

But what is the width of the blue union of the flag? Think about this for a second, because the answer soon becomes obvious. Remember the stripes. . . . That's right, the union is seven stripes wide, and all thirteen stripes are the same width. Therefore, the union is 7/13 (0.5385) the width of the flag. Its length is also 0.76 the width of the flag, a more arbitrary measurement.

PART TWO

The American Flag in Public Life

The Prominence of the Flag

IN OTHER WORDS

The United States flag must always be the most prominent flag or pennant flown. This is not an option. Prominence is indicated by either flying the flag higher than other flags or by flying the flag to the right of all other flags. "Right" refers to the flag's *own* right.

FOR EXAMPLE

Think of yourself as the flag. You are standing, facing an audience. If you are on the same level as other flags, instead of above them, those lesser flags will be on your left. If you look to your right, there is nothing there because you are in the position of prominence at the right-hand edge of the line of flags. In other words, you are positioned on the flag's own right and all the other flags are on the flag's own left. If you are in the audience, the American flag will therefore be positioned on the left.

ALSO

The American flag should be the largest flag flown or, at the very least, roughly the same size as the largest flag flown. Nobody's going to haul down two flags and measure them, as long as the other flag doesn't overshadow the American flag in any way.

WHY IS THIS?

The prominence of the American flag is one of the core tenets of flag display. This is symbolic of the fact that, at least on American soil, there is no authority higher than that of the government of the United States. That includes your state, city, business, or local civic group—and even your favorite college football team.

DID YOU KNOW?

The U.S. Constitution clearly states that there should be total separation between church and state. But which one is more prominent? In terms of the flag, the answer is the state. U.S. flags are flown above church flags on American soil.

The American flag should be flown with all other flags to its own left.

The Exceptions

There are only two exceptions to the rule that the American flag must always be flown in a position of prominence on American soil, both of which appear in Section 7(c) of the U.S. Flag Code.

The first is "during church services conducted by naval chaplains at sea, when the church pennant may be flown above the flag during church services for the personnel of the Navy." This is a temporary exemption, lasting only while the service is in progress.

The second exception states that nothing "shall make unlawful the continuance of the practice heretofore followed of displaying the flag of the United Nations in a position of superior prominence or honor, and other national flags in positions of equal prominence or honor, with that of the flag of the United States at the headquarters of the United Nations."

The United Nations is located on the banks of the East River in Manhattan. However, the eighteen-acre site is not *technically* on American soil; it is owned by the member states of the United Nations. This stipulation includes the beautiful plaza near the headquarters where the flags of all 188 member nations are flown in English alphabetical order, from Afghanistan to Zimbabwe.

The idea is that under the stewardship of a free and nonpartisan authority, all countries large and small are equal and united to promote the common good of mankind.

Respecting the Flag

IN OTHER WORDS

"Dipping" means lowering a handheld flag on a staff to at least a forty-five-degree angle from vertical, then raising it back to vertical. The flag should almost, but not quite, touch the ground in the lowered position. Dipping the flag is a mark of subjugation, a nodding of respect to a greater power. The code indicates that the American flag kneels in subjugation to no other flag; therefore, it is never dipped to another flag.

FOR EXAMPLE

State flags, and all other lesser flags, such as those of regiments or civic organizations, are dipped to the American flag when it passes. They are also dipped during the playing of "The Star-Spangled Banner." That is why, when a color guard presents flags before a rally or sporting event, all flags are lowered for the national anthem except the American flag, which is held high and aloft.

WHY IS THIS?

Dipping the flag is an old naval custom. It began hundreds of years ago when merchant ships were expected to clew up (take down) their topsails when approached by a man-of-war of a sovereign nation. The idea was that the merchant ship could not run effectively with its topsails down, guaranteeing that the man-of-war would be allowed to board and inspect her. This process was cumbersome, however, so the practice began of lowering the *ensign* (the name for a national flag flown from a ship) as a sign of acquiescence. Eventually, the practice became common at civilian events and with land armies, and today these groups still dip their regimental colors to the national flag.

DID YOU KNOW?

The American flag can be legally dipped on one occasion, but it happens only every four years. At the opening ceremony of the Olympics, the flags of all nations are dipped to foreign leaders, and the American flag is no exception.

The Pledge of Allegiance

IN OTHER WORDS

The Pledge of Allegiance should be read or recited only in the presence of the flag. Before it is read, everyone in attendance should stand and face the flag. If the flag is not visible, you should face its general direction.

FOR EXAMPLE

There is no need to make a scene when standing for the Pledge of Allegiance. If you have to crane to see the flag—for instance, if it is high overhead, around a corner, or behind a very large man—you should simply look in the flag's general direction. The pledge should be recited in unison by all in attendance. Mumbling or shouting is not encouraged.

ALSO

The Pledge of Allegiance is codified in U.S. Code, Title 36, Chapter 10, Section 172 in the section pertaining to the armed forces.

WHY IS THIS?

The United States is one of the few countries in the world that has an oath dedicated to its flag. We recite it, in the words of *Black's Law Dictionary*, as an acknowledgment of our "obligation of fidelity and obedience to government in consideration for the protections that society gives." This is probably the most obvious instance where the flag stands in as a proxy for country and government.

DID YOU KNOW?

The Pledge of Allegiance was written in 1892 by the magazine writers Francis Bellamy and James Upham for the official celebration of the four hundredth anniversary of Columbus's discovery of the New World. After it was published in Upham's magazine, *Youth's Companion*, the pledge became a national hit and was soon recited by schoolchildren before the start of each class day. In 1954, the words "under God" were added to the pledge by President Eisenhower after a vigorous public campaign led by the Knights of Columbus. A debate has raged ever since about the propriety of this religious message, given the separation of church and state that is the foundation of our government. The debate has culminated, for now, in the Ninth Circuit Court, the highest court in nine western states—the court ruled that the pledge is unconstitutional in 2002. The U.S. Supreme Court is currently set to review this ruling.

Saluting the Flag, Civilians

IN OTHER WORDS

Everyone in attendance should place his or her right hand on the heart when reciting the Pledge of Allegiance. Men should remove whatever is on their head. Women are not required or expected to remove their hats, visors, earmuffs, or other head coverings. Note that the hand, not the hat, should be over the heart.

FOR EXAMPLE

If you're a man and you're wearing a winter hat in subfreezing temperatures, you should remove it for the duration of the pledge. Your wife, however, can stay respectfully warm.

WHY IS THIS?

The United States is the first country to authorize a pledge to its flag. Similarly, this pledge was the first ritual created for civilians to collectively honor the country and the government. Therefore, a new form of salute, a civilian salute, had to be created to accompany it. The hand-on-heart symbol of honor is the civilian version of the military salute. Only those in uniform, either in active service, as veterans, or as a uniformed member of a civic organization like the Boy or Girl Scouts of America, may use the military salute.

DID YOU KNOW?

The civilian salute was created by the pledge's co-writer Francis Bellamy for the first reading of the Pledge of Allegiance in 1892. In his program for that year's Columbus Day celebration, Bellamy instructed children to stand with their hands at their sides, face the flag, and then give a military salute with "right hand lifted, palm downward, to a line with the forehead and close to it." At the words "to my flag," the children were instructed to extend the hand toward the flag, and then leave it in this extended position for the duration of the pledge. Unfortunately, this salute was very similar to the one adopted by the German Nazi party several decades later. The salute was changed to the hand-over-heart style in 1942.

Saluting the Flag, Military

IN OTHER WORDS

In a military salute, the right hand is brought horizontally to the forehead, but not quite touching the skin. It is a "one-count movement," meaning that there is no stopping or steps in the salute. The hand is simply brought to the forehead and then removed. This salute is reserved for members of the military.

FOR EXAMPLE

In many instances, police officers and firefighters in uniform are given the same reverence and treatment as military personnel. Not in this case. Civil servants are expected to use the civilian salute, as are active military personnel who are not in uniform (in other words, off duty).

WHY IS THIS?

No one knows the precise origin of the military salute. Since earliest times, the empty right hand (weapon hand) has been raised by military men to show that no weapon is hidden and no harm is intended. The salute probably developed from the age-old British tradition of removing your hat to a senior officer. As headgear became more advanced and cumbersome, this tradition grew more and more tedious. As early as 1745, a British order book stated that men were no longer to remove their hats to superior officers but "only to clasp up their hands to their hats and bow as they pass." Leave out the bowing, and you've got today's American military salute.

DID YOU KNOW?
The original military salute involved bringing both hands to one's head. This could get pretty hazardous if the junior officer was carrying something, and especially if that something were a sword. As recently as a hundred years ago, a left-handed salute was interchangeable with a right-handed salute in some cases. Unfortunately for lefties, this is no longer the case.

"The Star-Spangled Banner"

IN OTHER WORDS

"The Star-Spangled Banner" is not mentioned in the flag code itself, but it is recognized as the national anthem a few thousand pages later. The actions you should take for "The Star-Spangled Banner" are the same as those for the Pledge of Allegiance.

FOR EXAMPLE

If you're at an event, and they've got the pledge followed by the national anthem, just hang tight in your original salute and you'll be fine. You should not salute a foreign flag during its national anthem, but it is highly recommended that you remain silent and reverent during the entire ceremony.

WHY IS THIS?

Although national anthems became very popular in Europe starting in the mid-1800s, the United States did not have an official national anthem until 1931. Note the word "official." "The Star-Spangled Banner" became enormously popular as a patriotic hymn almost as soon as Francis Scott Key wrote it in 1814; essentially, it was the country's unofficial anthem. The song brought Key, a lawyer and aspiring poet, great fame and prosperity, but alas, he was never able to write anything nearly as widely recognized after that.

DID YOU KNOW?

The song we call "The Star-Spangled Banner" started life as a four-stanza poem called "The Defense of Fort McHenry." Francis Scott Key had no intention of setting the poem to music, but when it was printed, an unknown person—many believe it was Key's brother-in-law Joseph H. Nicholson—wrote the words "Anacreon in Heaven" on the top of the page. "Anacreon in Heaven" was the theme song of the Anacreonic Society, a drinking club that met regularly in a London pub to discuss philosophy and get sloshed. The song had become a popular drinking anthem across the pond in America, and its melody was adopted for what was to become our national anthem, "The Star-Spangled Banner."

The National Anthem

Most people know the story: During the War of 1812, a young lawyer named Francis Scott Key is aboard a British warship in the Chesapeake Bay negotiating the release of an American prisoner of war. As the British bombard Fort McHenry, an important American stronghold that guards the mouth of the port of Baltimore, Key is ordered to stay onboard during the battle. He watches over the ship's rampart (railing), and as night turns to dawn he sees the American flag still flying proudly over the besieged fort. As he starts to scribble a poem, an ode to the sight of that proud banner waving in the morning breeze, the British call off the attack. Key leaves the ship with the prisoner he came to release, and the first few lines of what would become his life's crowning achievement.

But what about the famous star-spangled flag that flew proudly over Fort McHenry? Just as Key was no ordinary lawyer, that banner was no ordinary flag. In fact, at 30 feet by 42 feet, it was then one of the largest flags ever made (although it is smaller than many flags that fly over gas stations today). It took the seamstress Mary Pickersgill and her daughter Caroline several weeks just to cut and prepare the numerous pieces. Because the flag was too large for her home, Pickersgill arranged to use space in a nearby brewery in order to stitch the flag together at night. For the entire job, Pickersgill was paid $405.90, a tidy sum at the time. Today, Mary Pickersgill's house—the Star-Spangled Banner House—serves as a Baltimore museum.

The flag, known as the Star-Spangled Banner, now hangs in the Smithsonian's National Museum of American History. If visitors look closely (or read the accompanying plaque), they will notice that the Star-Spangled Banner is one of those odd ducks that were only made for only about twenty years, between 1797 and 1818: an official American flag with fifteen stripes (see page 21).

Flags on Government Buildings, Polling Places, and Schools

IN OTHER WORDS

Public colleges and schools are the only nongovernmental buildings singled out by the code as places to fly the flag. Notice, however, that colleges and schools *should* fly the flag. In other words, flying the flag is recommended but not required. All government buildings *are* required to fly a United States flag.

FOR EXAMPLE

Many public schools, from elementary to high school, have a color guard to raise and lower the flag every morning. This is usually an honor bestowed upon the best and brightest of the students. However, kids being kids, it is often accompanied by taunting and bullying from less patriotic classmates.

ALSO

> THE FLAG SHALL BE DISPLAYED in or near every polling place on election days.
>
> *U.S. Code, Title 4, Chapter 1, Section 6(f)*

WHY IS THIS?

Public schools and colleges are owned by the government and, therefore, are part of our national infrastructure. It is not required that these institutions fly the flag, but it is strongly encouraged in order to, among other reasons, instill a sense of patriotism in the students. Notice, however, that the flag is required to be flown at polling places on Election Day. One reason is that the flag makes it easier for voters to know where to go in order to vote. A more fundamental reason is that the universal right to vote forms the basis of our government and is the bedrock upon which our nation rests, and the flying flag signals this fact.

DID YOU KNOW?

Prior to the Civil War, there is only one known instance of a schoolhouse flying a flag, and that took place in 1817. During the Civil War, however, every schoolhouse in the northern states began to fly a flag as a show of solidarity for the Union and the principles for which it stood. Flags have been flying from schoolhouses ever since.

The Flag in a Parade or a Procession

IN OTHER WORDS

The American flag must always be carried in the position of prominence. This means it must be at the front of any group, whether in a series of flags or among a high school marching band. In a line, the position on the far right (the *flag's* far right, see page 34) is the most prominent position. A flag in a procession must always be carried on a handheld staff.

The flag is carried on the far right (flag's own right; audience's left) during a parade or procession.

FOR EXAMPLE

If you are watching a parade of flags coming toward you, the American flag will always be the most visible flag because it will be the first in line. If there is a line of flags, the American flag will be on your far left. Only when you are carrying the flag, or are part of the group in which the flag is being carried, will the flag appear to be on the far right.

ALSO

There are only two correct ways for a single person to carry the flag in a procession. The first is to hold the end of a handheld staff at the waist (belt buckle) with the left hand at the base of the staff and right hand about two feet up the staff. Depending on the size of the staff and the flag, this can be physically difficult, which is why many people use a flag holder that ties around the waist and cradles the base of the staff.

The second option is to carry the staff tilted over the right shoulder, with the flag draping behind the carrier. In both instances, the flag must be allowed to hang freely. It should never touch the ground or any other object and should not be held at such an angle that it falls over the staff itself.

WHY IS THIS?

The tradition of carrying a flag at the front right derives from military usage. The flag, being the banner behind which troops rally, is usually carried at the front of a formation. (It is, however, sometimes kept in the back.) Since ancient Roman times, the right side of a military formation has always been the leading edge. The flag is therefore carried either in the center of the line or on the front right.

DID YOU KNOW?

The right side of a military formation is traditionally the strongest because most people are right-handed. This may not matter today, in an age of laser-guided missiles and smart bombs, but in Roman times the legions fought with swords in a tight cluster of bodies. Each soldier held his sword in his right hand and his shield in his left. This rendered the individual on the right end of the line more exposed than his comrades; thus, this position was taken by the strongest warrior. Being on the right leading edge of the formation soon became the place of honor in the legion.

The Flag on Public Transportation

THE CODE

THE FLAG SHOULD NOT BE DRAPED over the hood, top, sides, or back of a vehicle or of a railroad train or a boat.

U.S. Code, Title 4, Chapter 1, Section 7(b)

IN OTHER WORDS

Many public vehicles—buses, trains, boats, taxis, vans carrying church groups to the local amusement park—feature the American flag as a show of patriotism. However, the rule on displaying flags on public vehicles clearly states that this emblem should never be an *actual* American flag. For this reason, stickers featuring the flag have become very popular on public transportation. Unfortunately, these stickers often tend to peel and curl at the edges, defeating the whole purpose of devising a system that can keep the flag pure and undamaged. A discussion of the proper way to hang a flag from a car is on page 88.

Painted flags on the tail of American or U.S. government airlines depict the union on the right, as it would appear if it were an actual flag flying in the breeze.

Flags are never flown from airplanes since, clearly, they would be torn to bits by high-speed winds. However, all airplanes flown by the United States are affixed with a small painted flag on their right sides. Many people notice that these flags have the union in the upper right-hand corner. Is this a violation of the flag code? Not in this case, because if a picture of a flag is affixed to a moving vehicle, the image should be affixed so it appears that the flag is flying in the breeze. In other words, if there really were a flag on the side of an airplane, the fly end would be toward the rear, just as it is on the painted flag.

ALSO

THE FLAG SHOULD NOT BE DISPLAYED on a float in a parade except from a staff.

U.S. Code, Title 4, Chapter 1, Section 7(a)

WHY IS THIS?

There is no obscure flag law regarding the proper display of the flag on a railroad train or fast boat. The reasons are practical. Flags tend to fray or tear at high speeds, and squashed bugs, soot, and dirt do not honor the flag. The one exception to this rule is extremely slow-moving vehicles, like parade floats, which never move fast enough to damage the flag. In these cases, the flag must be flown from a staff and must be far enough from the float to fly free.

The proper *ensign* (boat-speak for flag) of any U.S. boat is Old Glory, with its fifty stars and thirteen stripes. However, a special Betsy Ross flag is often flown by American yachts. The union of the Betsy Ross flag contains thirteen stars, arranged in a circle, surrounding an anchor. Although this flag is often flown from recreational vehicles, it is never proper to use this flag in international or foreign waters. Old Glory should be used to identify any American boat outside of U.S. waters. And remember, if you're chasing criminals through Biscayne Bay in your cigarette boat, lower your flag, for as any good American knows, it is not proper to fly the flag while racing, chasing, or trying to elude capture.

Recreational boats and yachts navigating U.S. waters often display a special version of the Betsy Ross flag.

The Flag on Platforms and Stages

IN OTHER WORDS

When hanging your flag flat, rather than on a pole, it should be placed above and behind the speaker. If you are hanging the flag on a rear wall, it should be visible, and so it must be above the speaker. If you are displaying a flag on a staff, the place of honor is behind the speaker and *to the speaker's right*. If you are sitting in the audience facing the speaker, the flag will be to his left. Other flags should be to the speaker's left, or, if you are looking from the audience, to the right.

FOR EXAMPLE

In any display from a platform, if you are in the audience and the flag appears on the left, chances are it is being displayed correctly. Remember that when the flag is hung flat behind a speaker, the union should be on the flag's own right, whether the flag is hung vertically or horizontally. From the audience, the flag will appear above the speaker, and the union will appear on the upper left-hand corner of the flag.

WHY IS THIS?

It is believed that the flag is flown to the right of the speaker as a sign of peace. At one time, the right hand was synonymous with the weapon hand. The right hand without a weapon indicates that no harm is intended.

DID YOU KNOW?

The movie Patton opens with General George S. Patton striding out in front of a backdrop of an enormous American flag and delivering a speech that rouses his troops. The visual image is one of the most memorable in movie history, and it shows the beauty and power of the American flag when used as a backdrop to a speech (in this case it was not above the general, but filled the whole screen). General Patton did deliver that speech, and it did rouse his troops, but movie history doesn't reflect U.S. history exactly. General Patton's actual speech, if spoken by George C. Scott in the film, would have probably given the film an adults-only rating. General Patton rallied his troops with the language of a tough field commander—speech not intended for the faint of heart. And as far as we know, there was no enormous American flag hung directly behind him at the time.

The Flag in Public Buildings

THE CODE

WHEN THE FLAG IS SUSPENDED ACROSS a corridor or lobby in a building with only one main entrance, it should be suspended vertically with the union of the flag to the observer's left upon entering. If the building has more than one main entrance, the flag should be suspended vertically near the center of the corridor or lobby with the union to the north, when entrances are to the east and west or to the east when entrances are to the north and south. If there are entrances in more than two directions, the union should be to the east.

U.S. Code, Title 4, Chapter 1, Section 7(o)

IN OTHER WORDS

When a flag is suspended in an entrance to a building, it is displayed vertically, that is, stripes hanging straight up and down with the union at the top. If there is only one main entrance, orienting the flag is easy—the union should be on the flag's own right, the viewer's left. If there is more than one main entrance, as in the case of many large office buildings and shopping areas, hanging the flag is a bit more complicated. In fact, you'll need a compass. The orientation depends upon where those entrances are. If the entrances are to the north and south, the flag should face the north entrance because that would put the union on the east. If the entrances are to the east and west, the flag should face the west entrance, so that the union is on the north. If the entrances are in more than two directions, the flag should face the north with the union to the east.

FOR EXAMPLE

In a corridor or lobby with four or more entrances (such as a rotunda), the flag should be hung as near as possible to the center of the room. Get a compass, find east, and hang the flag straight up and down so that the flag is facing north and the union is to the east—even if there is not an entrance facing due north!

WHY IS THIS?

As always, the union should be on the flag's own right (the left side if you are facing the flag). But when someone approaches the flag from the back, as they might if the building has two separate entrances, it appears as if the union is on the flag's own left. This was an impossible dilemma. Therefore, a standard direction was needed. Should the flag always face the capital? This didn't seem appropriate or possible. Was there a direction that signified, somehow, America? Not really. It was therefore decided that the union should appear on the east, the direction of the rising sun.

DID YOU KNOW?

For a spectacular example of a correct display of the American flag, visitors can see the original Star-Spangled Banner displayed in the entrance hall to the National Museum of American History's mall entrance, right next to the Foucault pendulum.

The Flag at Statue and Monument Unveilings

IN OTHER WORDS

At a statue or unveiling ceremony, the American flag should be displayed to the right of the statue or monument. From the perspective of the audience, the flag would be on the left. The flag should never cover what is being unveiled—that's the job of a regular cloth or shroud—but should instead fly freely.

FOR EXAMPLE

If you're unveiling a patriotic statue on a patriotic holiday like Veteran's Day or the Fourth of July, it is appropriate to cover a statue with red, white, and blue coverings, such as bunting (see page 109) and ribbons, but not with an actual flag.

WHY IS THIS?

There are two concepts at play here. The first is that the flag should always have a position of prominence. If the flag were used to cover the statue, the statue, rather than the flag, would be the prominent feature. The second is that the flag should always fly free and unhindered. If it were draped over the statue, it would be lying limp, bound, and entirely hindered.

Although the American flag should not be draped over a statue at its unveiling, there is nothing wrong with having the American flag be a part of the statue itself. In fact, one of the most famous and moving statues commemorating the soldiers of World War II is the Marine Corps War Memorial in Arlington, Virginia. This sculpture depicts U.S. soldiers raising the U.S. flag at Iwo Jima. Sculptor Felix de Weldon based the sculpture on an actual photo of that glorious moment on Mount Suribachi. Although the statue itself is cast in bronze, the flagpole of the statue supports an actual American flag, flown twenty-four hours a day.

The Flag on Caskets

THE CODE

WHEN THE FLAG IS USED TO COVER A CASKET, it should be so placed that the union is at the head and over the left shoulder. The flag should not be lowered into the grave or allowed to touch the ground.

U.S. Code, Title 4, Chapter 1, Section 7(n)

IN OTHER WORDS

Flag-draped coffins are reserved for military veterans and those, such as government functionaries, who died in the service of their country. In this ceremony, the flag is spread to cover the entire coffin during the funeral, with the union in the upper left corner. Once the procession reaches the burial site, the flag is lifted off the coffin and folded. This is to prevent the flag from touching the ground.

FOR EXAMPLE

President John F. Kennedy rested in state beneath a flag-draped coffin not only because he was killed serving his country as president, but also because he was a military veteran. The image of President Kennedy's procession, with his son's salute to the flag-draped coffin, is one of the most memorable in our nation's history.

WHY IS THIS?

The tradition of draping a body with the flag started in the Napoleonic Wars of the late eighteenth century, when the soldiers of many nations came together on the battlefield to fight the French advance. Wounded soldiers of that era were borne from the field on a caisson and left at the rear of the fighting. If their wounds proved mortal, their remains were covered with their national flag until burial, at which time the flag was removed. Today, the flag-draped coffin remains a sign of respect for the bravery of a soldier, even if that soldier died in the quiet of his or her own home, decades after his or her service.

DID YOU KNOW?

Many churches, and in particular the Catholic Church, require the removal of the flag from the coffin before it enters the sanctuary to signify that nothing, even the flag and the country for which it stands, comes between the saved soul and God.

The Military Funeral

The coffins of military veterans are, if the family so chooses, covered in the flag of the United States of America as a symbol of their valiant service. The flag is draped over the casket once it is closed and in a civilian service it remains until the end of the funeral or, if the funeral is held in certain churches, until just before the casket enters the sanctuary.

In the case of military funerals at national cemeteries, the flag-draped coffin is brought to the burial site. The rifle squad then fires three volleys, a tradition that began as the signal to halt a battle so that the dead could be removed from the field and given proper burial. In the modern ceremony, the rifle volleys symbolize that the deceased has been removed from life's field of battle.

After the third rifle volley has died away, a bugler plays taps (or a recording is played). Taps, based on an old French bugle call, was first used by Brigadier General Daniel Butterfield to bury fallen soldiers at the Battle of Harrison's Landing, Virginia, in 1862. It was quickly adopted by both Union and Confederate soldiers and eventually became an official part of military funerals in 1874.

The American flag is then gently lifted from the coffin by a squad of three persons, two of whom fold the flag in the precise, thirteen-fold manner used by the U.S. Armed Forces. Once it is folded, the third person carries the flag from the grave and presents it to the deceased's next of kin.

A military funeral with a flag-draped coffin, at least two persons on active military duty, and a recording of taps is guaranteed to all honorably discharged veterans by Title 10, Chapter 2, Section 1491 of the U.S. Code.

PART THREE

Caring For and Displaying
Your American Flag

The Proper Days to Display the Flag

THE FLAG SHALL BE DISPLAYED ON ALL DAYS, especially on New Year's Day, January 1; Inauguration Day, January 20; Martin Luther King Jr.'s Birthday, third Monday in January; Lincoln's Birthday, February 12; Washington's Birthday, third Monday in February; Easter Sunday (variable); Mother's Day, second Sunday in May; Armed Forces Day, third Saturday in May; Memorial Day (half-staff until noon), the last Monday in May; Flag Day, June 14; Independence Day, July 4; Labor Day, first Monday in September; Constitution Day, September 17; Columbus Day, second Monday in October; Navy Day, October 27; Veteran's Day, November 11; Thanksgiving Day, fourth Thursday in November; Christmas Day, December 25; and such other days as may be proclaimed by the President of the United States; the birthdays of states (date of admission); and on State holidays.

U.S. Code, Title 4, Chapter 1, Section 6(d)

IN OTHER WORDS

If you own a flag, you are permitted and encouraged to fly it three hundred sixty-five days a year, weather permitting. You are strongly encouraged to fly it on those days that are special to the history of our country. No one is *required* to fly a flag on these days, of course, but if you own a flag you may especially enjoy flying it on these occasions.

FOR EXAMPLE

Many people dust off their flags a couple of times a year for patriotic holidays such as the Fourth of July and Flag Day. Fewer people bring out the flag on days such as Thanksgiving Day, although according to the flag code there is nothing more or less patriotic about this holiday than any of the others.

ALSO

President George W. Bush added September 11 to the list of days on which Americans are encouraged to fly the flag. In a presidential proclamation, the president encouraged Americans to fly the flag at half-mast, stating: "We will not forget the events of that terrible morning nor will we forget how Americans responded in New York City, at the Pentagon, and in the skies over Pennsylvania—with heroism and selflessness; with compassion and courage; and with prayer and hope." On December 18, 2001, Congress passed a resolution authorizing the president to designate September 11 of each year as Patriot Day.

WHY IS THIS?

The listed holidays may seem a bit odd at first. Certainly Independence Day, Veteran's Day, and Memorial Day make sense. But Mother's Day and Christmas, while special and meaningful to many Americans, aren't really patriotic holidays. Nevertheless, the listed holidays are meant to symbolize those days that are significant to Americans—not just noteworthy to the country, but special to the character of many Americans themselves. So if the emotion moves you, feel free to add any days that are special to your traditions to the list of days when you fly your flag.

DID YOU KNOW?

In the aftermath of the attacks on the United States on September 11, 2001, many people who had never before hoisted a flag began to display their flags regularly. Unfortunately, flying the flag produced controversies in several states and cities when condominium boards or homeowners' associations objected to exterior decorations, including flags. Some state and local legislatures have intervened and produced laws to override the rules of these groups. In California, for instance, Governor Gray Davis signed legislation in 2002 that allows homeowners to fly flags above their homes regardless of any rules passed by homeowners' associations.

The Flag's Birthday

On June 14, 1777, the Second Continental Congress authorized the use of a new flag to symbolize the newly formed United States of America. At the time, the flag consisted of thirteen stripes, alternating red and white, and a union of thirteen white stars on a blue field. Although Congress changed the flag several times between 1777 and 1960, June 14 is considered the "birthday" of the original American flag.

Before there was a national Flag Day, the anniversary of the creation of the flag was commemorated at different times in different jurisdictions. Hartford, Connecticut, celebrated a flag day in June 1861, the first summer of the American Civil War. In 1885, a Wisconsin schoolteacher asked his pupils to celebrate June 14 as the birthday of the American flag. A New York schoolteacher followed his lead in 1889. Soon, a movement had spread throughout the United States calling for a national observance of the birthday of the American flag.

In 1916, while World War I raged in Europe and Africa, President Woodrow Wilson issued a proclamation asking Americans to observe Flag Day on June 14. It was not until 1949, however, that Congress passed a resolution, signed by President Harry S. Truman, designating June 14 of each year as Flag Day.

Flag Day is not a federal holiday, and very few people get a day off of work or school for the occasion, yet it remains a special day on which Americans are encouraged to fly the flag and celebrate its meaning.

The Proper Time to Display the Flag

IN OTHER WORDS

Your flag should be flown outdoors only for a set period of time, for example, nine in the morning to six at night on a holiday. Unless you have a light *dedicated* to illuminating your flag after dark, your flag should be flown only during the day. Flying a flag in a lit area is not sufficient. With proper illumination, a flag may be flown twenty-four hours a day for as many consecutive days as you like, weather permitting.

FOR EXAMPLE

Flag-raising and -lowering ceremonies are commonplace throughout the United States and the world, and you can show the same respect for the flag when raising and lowering it at home. Watching, or even participating in, the raising and lowering of the flag is a rite of passage for summer campers throughout the country. Some families even invite neighbors for their flag-raising ceremony on the Fourth of July.

ALSO

The custom of displaying the flag over the east and west fronts of the U.S. Capitol Building twenty-four hours a day began during World War I by popular request. Presidential proclamations and laws require that the flag be flown twenty-four hours a day at the following locations: Fort McHenry National Monument and Historic Shrine, Baltimore, Maryland; Flag House Square, Baltimore, Maryland; United States Marine Corps War Memorial, Arlington, Virginia; on the green of the town of Lexington, Massachusetts; the White House, Washington, D.C.; the United States Customs ports of entry; and the grounds of the National Memorial Arch in Valley Forge State Park, Valley Forge, Pennsylvania.

WHY IS THIS?

It is important not only to fly the flag but also to be an active participant in its flying. Shining a light on your flag at night is one way to show this respect. A better way is to take the time and care to raise your flag each morning and to lower it each night. This way flying the flag becomes a part of your daily life, and not just something you spend a few minutes doing once and then forget about until someone points out that your flag is torn, soiled, or wrapped around its pole.

DID YOU KNOW?

Limiting the display of national flags from sunrise to sunset is not unique to the United States. Nations from China to Denmark customarily raise flags at sunup and lower them at sundown. Why? Because raising the flag each morning is a powerful symbol of national identity. After the United Kingdom returned Hong Kong to mainland China in 1997, daily flag-raising ceremonies were instituted on Bauhinia Square, a location readily accessible to tourists and locals alike. The ceremony was meant to reinforce a Chinese, rather than British, identity among the citizens of Hong Kong.

The Proper Weather to Display the Flag

IN OTHER WORDS

Unless you've invested in an all-weather flag, don't leave your flag out in rain, snow, sleet, or other inclement weather. It's not as durable as the postman, you know!

FOR EXAMPLE

This rule may seem almost obsolete, as most flags produced today are considered "all weather." Modern flags are waterproof and resistant to tearing, wearing, and stains. A quick survey of your neighborhood, however, will probably reveal a flag or two in sorry condition. Although technically it is correct to display an all-weather flag in any weather, it is a good idea to bring your flag indoors if severe weather threatens to damage your flag.

WHY IS THIS?

The reason for this rule is simple—bad weather conditions damage flags. A damaged flag may actually be a sign of *disrespect* to the nation it represents. A tattered, torn, and streaked flag is not a sign of a patriotic citizen.

Although your American flag should not be displayed in inclement weather, it has been displayed in some pretty adverse conditions. In 1969, the flag of the United States was displayed on the moon. There's no rain or sleet on the moon but there's also very little gravity, and therefore no way for it to "fly." For this reason, a wire was run across the top of the flag to make it appear to be flying free.

The only place on earth with more inhospitable conditions than the moon may be the North Pole. You guessed it, the flag's been there, too. In 1909, Robert Peary, Matthew Henson, and four Inuit guides sought to be the first men to reach the North Pole and plant the American flag into the icy ground. Although Peary is often credited as the first man to reach the Pole, his companion Henson, an African American, actually reached it first and planted the flag. Conditions were overcast and frigid at the time the flag was planted, but Henson can be forgiven for flying his flag in inclement weather because of the monumental importance of where and when this flag was flown.

What of a second flag brought on the trip by Peary? It seems the intrepid adventurer cut that flag to pieces and left it scattered at the North Pole. Although cutting the American flag to pieces would usually be considered an act of desecration, Peary can be excused for this flagrant code breaking because, well, he had a very good reason: it took Peary several attempts to reach the Pole, so to mark his progress he left a small piece of the flag behind each time he turned back.

Fringed Flags

Conspiracy theorists have always been attracted to the fringe, so to speak. For years, diverse and often contradictory rumors have swirled around the use of a gold fringe on the American flag. The fringe is believed by some to symbolize the gold standard for U.S. currency; to others it indicates that the United States or a specific court is under martial law; others believe it is the secret sign of anti-American conspirators.

    The truth is a bit less exciting. The U.S. Code makes no mention of fringe on the flag. In 1925, the U.S. attorney general suggested that the fringe is not an integral part of the flag but also that it is *not* an unauthorized addition to the flag. In other words, although it is not acceptable to add something to the body of the flag itself, there is nothing wrong with using a gold or yellow fringe around the border of the flag. The fringe is a decorative addition, nothing more, and if a person wants to add a fringe to his flag, he isn't sending any message other than the fact that he likes a bit of added decoration.

The National Color flag.

    There is one official use for fringed flags in United States military regulations. In the U.S. Army, a fringe is added to what is called the National Color, a flag used indoors or carried on parade. These regulations apply only to the U.S. Army. The fact that the fringed flag is used in other situations does not make such a flag a U.S. military flag, so do not fear if you enter a court to contest your traffic tickets and see a fringed flag. That court is not under martial law, and you are still in the United States. You just happen to be in a courtroom where whoever is in charge of ordering the flags has an eye for decorative flair.

Raising and Lowering the Flag

IN OTHER WORDS

When using a flagpole, your flag should be raised swiftly but without rushing or pulling in a jerky, uneven manner. It should be lowered slowly, at a steady speed.

FOR EXAMPLE

It should take approximately twenty seconds to raise a flag to the top of a standard thirty-foot flagpole. The lowering of the flag should take about sixty seconds.

WHY IS THIS?

The goal in any flag ceremony is always to have the flag flying free and unfettered. It is therefore imperative to get the flag out of your hands and flying as quickly as possible. Any admiration of the flag should be done when the flag is at full mast. The lowering of your flag is a more formal occasion. It should be lowered slowly both to show the reluctance at lowering the emblem of our country and to give the participants time to contemplate the meaning of the flag.

DID YOU KNOW?

The ceremony of raising the flag, and the image of a rising flag blowing in the breeze, evokes such strong feelings among Americans that the Library of Congress regularly includes this theme when choosing images for its *American Treasures* exhibition, which features historically significant items.

Flagpoles at Home

It's one thing to display an American flag, but it's another to invest in a flagpole. This is the ultimate way to show your patriotism and impress your neighbors. But be warned: you do need to check your local rules and regulations prior to making your purchase. Many of the flagpoles on Long Island, New York, for instance, were removed in the 1990s because they were set too close to roads and sidewalks. The authorities feared, with good reason, that an improperly supported or rusted pole could fall into the street and injure pedestrians.

A flagpole isn't just a stick in the ground. It is a potentially dangerous falling object that comes in a variety of materials and styles, and with an endless variety of accessories. You can buy poles in fiberglass, aluminum, bronze, or several other materials. None of these materials is correct or incorrect; it's all a matter of personal preference.

Now get out your notepad and pen, because that pole comes with quite a few extras. The *halyard* is the rope or cord used to raise or lower the flag. The *cleat* is the device near the bottom of the pole used to secure the halyard in place. The *truck* or *truck assembly* is the pulley mechanism at the top of the pole over which the halyard circles when raising or lowering the flag. The *finial* is the decorative piece, such as an eagle or ball, at the top of the pole.

The size of the flag displayed should be proportionate to the flagpole. A good general rule is that the horizontal length of the flag should be a quarter the length of the flagpole. Since most residential flags measure three by five feet, the pole height with which to display them would be twenty feet, although a shorter fifteen-foot pole is also considered appropriate for residential use.

The finial of a flagpole has generated many legends. One story popular during the 1950s held that the finials housed lighters or other devices that an American would find helpful in destroying the flag during a Soviet invasion, thus preventing the communists from desecrating it. Other stories hold that a bullet may be hidden in the finial. Like those surrounding the fringe of the flag, these stories are just urban legends. Think about it: in the unlikely event that the Soviets were parading through Boise, how would a patriotic American even reach the finial? Like many such legends, these stories sound interesting until the listener actually thinks them through. The fringe doesn't indicate martial law, and your finial doesn't have a lighter in it unless you put it there. Which is not recommended.

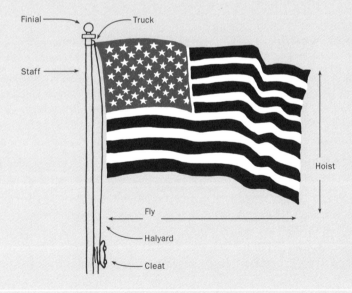

The Flag at Half-Staff

THE FLAG, WHEN FLOWN AT HALF-STAFF, should be first hoisted to the peak for an instant and then lowered to the half-staff position. The flag should be raised again to the peak before it is lowered for the day . . . the term "half-staff" means the position of the flag when it is one-half the distance between the top and bottom of the staff.

U.S. Code, Title 4, Chapter 1, Section 7(m) and (m)(1)

IN OTHER WORDS

At times of national mourning, the flag is flown at "half-staff" or "half-mast," a position one half the distance between the top and bottom of the flagpole. Before a flag is flown at half-staff, it should be briefly raised to the top of the pole. Before lowering the flag at the end of the day, it should be raised again to the top.

FOR EXAMPLE

Flags are flown at half-staff on days of national mourning, such as when a president or a vice president dies, on certain national holidays that commemorate the patriotic sacrifices of our citizens, and at times of national disaster.

WHY IS THIS?

The tradition of flying flags at half-mast probably originated on a ship, the mast being the part of the ship where the flag is hung. The history of the symbolism of this flag position is not entirely clear, but today it indicates mourning, much as someone might lower his or her head for a passing funeral procession. It has been suggested that flying the flag at half-mast is similar to tearing clothes or rubbing ashes on a person's skin—deliberately appearing disheveled to show grief—or that the flag flying at half-mast is meant to symbolize something missing above the flag. Whatever the origin, the custom is common worldwide.

DID YOU KNOW?

The earliest recorded instance of a flag flying at half-mast was in 1612. The commander of the exploring ship *Heart's Ease* was killed by native Inuit while trying to find the mythical Northwest Passage through North America to the Far East. His vessel flew its flag over the stern at half-mast, indicating that the commander had died. When the ship rejoined the others traveling with it, this position of the flag was immediately recognized as a sign of mourning for the commander; therefore, the tradition must have preceded this event and was likely common practice by this time.

The Flag on Memorial Day

IN OTHER WORDS

On Memorial Day, the flag should be raised briskly to the top of the flagpole, then lowered slowly to halfway down the pole. At noon, the flag is raised once more to the top of the flagpole.

FOR EXAMPLE

Veterans' groups throughout the country host Memorial Day ceremonies and commemorations. Far from being just a day off to visit the beach or have a picnic, Memorial Day is an opportunity to commemorate those who made the ultimate sacrifice for their country. For those who have served in the armed forces, this is a solemn day indeed.

ALSO

THE FLAG SHALL BE FLOWN AT HALF-STAFF on Peace Officers Memorial Day, unless that day is also Armed Forces Day.

U.S. Code, Title 4, Chapter 1, Section 7(m)

WHY IS THIS?

Memorial Day, initially called Decoration Day, is a holiday commemorating American soldiers who died serving their country. For this reason, the flag is flown at half-staff on this day. Originally, the holiday was observed by decorating the graves of soldiers with garlands and flowers; the Tomb of the Unknown Soldier is still decorated with wreaths in honor of their memories. It is now more common, however, to place small flags on the graves of our fallen military men and women. At Arlington National Cemetery, each grave receives a small flag on Memorial Day. When viewed in total, this is a stirring sight.

DID YOU KNOW?

You may have noticed veterans' groups handing out small paper flowers on Memorial Day. This tradition originates from the poem "In Flanders Fields," written by John McCrae in 1915 to honor the dead of World War I. The poem begins: "In Flanders Fields the poppies blow/ Between the crosses, row on row,/ That mark our place, and in the sky/ The larks, still bravely singing, fly/ Scarce heard amid the guns below." Distributing paper flowers is not simply a fund-raising effort. The flowers represent poppies, symbolic of the men who died for their country, and are intended to make us reflect on their sacrifices.

The Death of Government Officials

BY ORDER OF THE PRESIDENT, the flag shall be flown at half-staff upon the death of principal figures of the United States Government and the Governor of a State, territory, or possession, as a mark of respect to their memory. In the event of the death of other officials or foreign dignitaries, the flag is to be displayed at half-staff according to Presidential instructions or orders, or in accordance with recognized customs or practices not inconsistent with law. . . . The flag shall be flown at half-staff 30 days from the death of the President or a former President; 10 days from the death of the Vice President, the Chief Justice or a retired Chief Justice of the United States, or the Speaker of the House of Representatives; from the day of death until interment of an Associate Justice of the Supreme Court, a Secretary of an executive or military department, a former Vice President, or the Governor of a State, territory, or possession; and on the day of death and the following day of a Member of Congress.

U.S. Code, Title 4, Chapter 1, Section 7(m)

IN OTHER WORDS

The flag is to fly at half-staff when the nation is in mourning, as a mark of respect. The president has the authority to declare that all flags be flown at half-staff, although many of the occasions and their durations have already been decided. The flag is flown at half-staff for thirty days for the president or a former president, but only for the day of death and the following day for a member of Congress.

FOR EXAMPLE

After the disaster that killed several astronauts aboard the space shuttle *Columbia* in 2003, President George W. Bush issued a proclamation honoring each of those killed and ordered flags to be flown at half-staff over all federal buildings until the Wednesday following the accident, a total of four days.

ALSO

Since governors are the top officials of their states, the code allows for an extended display of reverence by the states.

WHY IS THIS?

It's only fitting that the flag should be flown at half-staff as a memorial to our fallen leaders. But for whom, exactly? And for how long? No regulations existed until 1954, when President Dwight Eisenhower issued a proclamation declaring the proper occasions and times.

DID YOU KNOW?

A death does not have to be recent to be commemorated by flying flags at half-staff. On December 14, 1999, President Bill Clinton ordered that flags be flown at half-staff to commemorate the two hundredth anniversary of the death of George Washington.

Folding the Flag

There are no code provisions governing the folding of the flag once it is removed from a flag-pole or staff. But since there is a rule that the flag should never be carried flat, folding is required. There is, therefore, a traditional method that will produce fine, triangular bundle that is neat, beautiful, and ready to be stored (which we'll learn about later on page 102).

1. Hold your flag parallel to the ground.
2. Bring up the bottom, striped half over the union half of the flag, folding lengthwise.
3. Fold the flag again lengthwise, with the union on the outside.
4. Make a triangular fold by bringing the striped edge up to the top of the flag.
5. Continue folding down the length of your flag, making triangular folds until a neat triangle results. If you have folded your flag correctly, nothing but the blue union should show.

The folding of the U.S. flag should take thirteen folds: two lengthwise folds and eleven triangular folds.

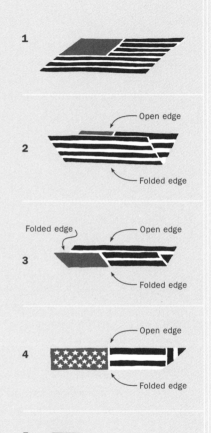

The Flag on a Staff

IN OTHER WORDS

The flagstaff is a common way for homeowners to display their flag because it is easier and less expensive to attach a staff to a home than erecting a pole in the front yard. Because flagstaffs are so common, however, abuse in the display of the flag at home is common. When attaching the staff to the house, it is a good idea to use a bracket to secure your staff and fasten it well. Be sure to hang the staff in a place where your flag is unlikely to be soiled, damaged, or entangled. And, always ensure that the union of your flag touches the very top of your staff.

FOR EXAMPLE

A staff should be twice as long as the flag flown upon it, and should be inserted into a bracket at a forty-five-degree angle, with the union at the top. This allows your flag to fly free—except when the wind wraps the flag around the staff itself. Flag owners should always be vigilant about this and other signs of flag irregularities. When your flag is wrapped around a dirty fire escape, tangled in a tree branch, or draped in the gutter with wet leaves and dirt, it doesn't honor our country.

ALSO

If multiple flags are displayed on the same staff, the U.S. flag should be upper-most, with the union at the peak of the staff.

WHY IS THIS?

Again, displaying your American flag at the top of the staff is a sign of respect. The union should be at the peak so that it will be uppermost on the staff and so the flag will fly freely. Don't worry about whether the union is being viewed from the front or from the back. As long as the union is at the peak of the staff, your flag is being flown correctly.

DID YOU KNOW?

You may be used to seeing flagstaffs hanging from every home in your neighborhood, but use of flags by individuals was not always so common. In its early days, the flag was most commonly used by the government, often for naval or military purposes, though ordinary citizens did occasionally fly the flag. During the Civil War, it became much more common for ordinary citizens (in the North) to fly the flag at home in order to show support for the Union. The display of the American flag by individuals remained popular after the Civil War, and almost a hundred years later, after the attack on Pearl Harbor and during the 1950s Cold War era, the white front porch flying an American flag became a symbol of "Main Street, America." Many people still think of a flag on a staff in front of an immaculate white porch as the very essence of Americana.

The Flag Suspended

IN OTHER WORDS

Believe it or not, hanging a flag properly over your street will require a compass! First, determine whether the street is oriented east to west or north to south. This might be difficult if yours is a curvy street, but use your best judgment. The flag should hang vertically, with the union at the top. On an east-west street, the union should point to the north. On a north-south street, the union should point to the east.

FOR EXAMPLE

Just as they hang Christmas lights in December, towns suspend flags over main streets as a patriotic display on Memorial Day. The incidences of *individuals* hanging flags across streets is very rare and, in many locations, illegal, due to civic safety concerns.

WHEN THE FLAG IS SUSPENDED OVER A SIDEWALK from a rope extending from a house to a pole at the edge of the sidewalk, the flag should be hoisted out, union first, from the building.

U.S. Code, Title 4, Chapter 1, Section 7(h)

WHY IS THIS?

When a flag is suspended over a street or a sidewalk, it is not possible to position the union on the flag's own right because the flag has two sides. From one direction, the flag would be oriented correctly, but from the other direction the flag would appear to be backwards. And even on a one-way street, walkers and joggers will approach the flag from both sides. Therefore, the flag is oriented by a compass, so that it will be positioned correctly no matter where the observer stands.

DID YOU KNOW?

Although it is common to see American flags suspended over streets or sidewalks in celebration of holidays, Waterloo, New York, carries things a bit further. The village, with a population of 5,118, set the world record for the most American flags flying in a town on May 29, 2000, when the inhabitants simultaneously sent 25,898 flags into the air (on staffs and poles, of course). Although one may suspect that there are more flags flown in New York City on a typical Fourth of July, even a large group of people would be hard-pressed to accurately count them all. Therefore, in this instance, New York City has met its Waterloo.

The Flag Against a Wall or Window

IN OTHER WORDS

When hanging your flag flat against a wall, the union should be at the top and on the flag's own right. To an observer, the union will be on the left. This is basic—until you consider a "wall" made of glass. In other words, a window or a glass wall. That's when most people stumble into a code violation. When the wall is a window, turn the flag around so that it is correctly viewed from the *outside*, not the inside.

FOR EXAMPLE

American flag decals are designed so that the flag will be in the correct position when viewed from the street. The flag may appear backwards to you as you affix it to your window, but from the perspective of the observer on the street the flag will be "hanging" correctly.

When hanging your flag on an interior wall, you hang it for yourself. When you hang a flag on a window, you hang it for outside viewing.

DID YOU KNOW?

As previously discussed (see page 47), Mary Pickersgill's home in Baltimore, Maryland (the Star-Spangled Banner House), now serves as a museum. What you may not know, unless you've been there recently, is that the museum has expanded, building a 30- by 42-foot "great flag window." The window is the same size, color, and design as the famous battle flag made by Mary Pickersgill. The flag is not affixed to the window of this patriotic museum: the flag *is* the window.

The Flag on Private Cars

THE CODE

THE FLAG SHOULD NOT BE DRAPED over the hood, top, sides, or back of a vehicle....When the flag is displayed on a motorcar, the staff shall be fixed firmly to the chassis or clamped to the right fender.

U.S. Code, Title 4, Chapter 1, Section 7(b)

IN OTHER WORDS

When displaying a flag from your car, the staff should be attached securely to the *front right* of the car, at either the *chassis* or the *bumper*. Next time you see a government motorcade, notice where the flags are positioned and you will know where to place the staff of your own flag.

FOR EXAMPLE

Tying your flag to the antenna, spare tire, luggage rack, or trailer hitch may seem like an easy solution to placing a flag on your car, but it is not the correct way to display your flag. Similarly, using a plastic staff that attaches to the edge of your car window is a great way to show pride in your sports team, but not your American flag.

WHY IS THIS?

A secure staff on the front right bumper or the chassis is ideal for the relatively slow pace of city driving. Plus, as you can still observe in old war movies and classic documentary footage, it looks really cool. But let's be honest: this technique isn't really appropriate for highway driving. These days, flags are clipped all over our cars and, unfortunately, many of them are ratty and neglected. If you wish to place a flag on your car, there are really only two acceptable ways: the bumper method listed on the opposite page or a flag decal on the window.

DID YOU KNOW?

Although William McKinley was the first president to ride in a car, the first president to travel in a government-owned car was Theodore Roosevelt. One photograph of Roosevelt traveling in his motorcade shows him standing up, hands on hips, gazing at the crowd. The staff of his automobile's flag is securely and correctly attached to the right bumper but, unfortunately, the flag is so large that it drapes over the hood of the car and the right front tire. This is not only hazardous to the flag; it's also a violation of the code, although it is understood that President Roosevelt served almost fifty years before this code was adopted into law.

Positioning the American Flag When Flown with Flags of Other Nations

IN OTHER WORDS

No flag of another nation, or of the United Nations, should be placed in a position of prominence or honor over the American flag. If you are an Italian American, for example, it is acceptable to fly the Italian flag along with Old Glory, but the United States flag should be flown in the position of prominence (to the American flag's own right, see page 34).

FOR EXAMPLE

The Six Flags amusement park chain, which operates parks serving thirty-five major U.S. metropolitan areas, as well as parks in Europe, began with a single park in Texas. The "Six Flags" name refers to the six flags that have flown over the state of Texas during its history: those of Spain, France, Mexico, the Republic of Texas, the Confederate States of America, and the current flag of the United States. Although the parks may display these flags, the U.S. flag should always fly in the position of prominence (but not above) in relation to the other flags.

ALSO

Government embassies are technically located on the soil of the foreign govern-
ments that they represent, even within the United States. For this reason,
embassies and consulates are allowed to fly their home country flags in the position of prominence. The same is true at United Nations headquarters, which is
technically a small patch of soil owned by the member states, even though this
soil is located in Manhattan.

WHY IS THIS?

Inside the border of a nation, that nation and its government rule above all others. Everyone in the world must respect that, even Americans living in, say,
Myanmar or Australia. Therefore, on that soil, that country's flag must be placed
above the American flag.

DID YOU KNOW?

When U.S. Navy ships are in foreign waters or saluting a foreign country, they fly
the flag of that country at the masthead of the ship. If the ship is under way, the
foreign flag may be above the U.S. flag, which is displayed at the stern or the gaff.
This practice might seem to violate the U.S. Code, but it does not. First, the code
is applicable to U.S. civilians, not to the U.S. Navy. Second, the code states that the
foreign flag should not be in a position of prominence to the U.S. flag. The code
does not say that the foreign flag may not be *above* the American flag in international waters. On a ship, the stern or the gaff is the position of prominence, not
the masthead.

Using Staffs When Flying the American Flag with Flags of Other Nations

THE CODE

WHEN FLAGS OF TWO OR MORE NATIONS ARE DISPLAYED, they are to be flown from separate staffs of the same height. The flags should be of approximately equal size. International usage forbids the display of the flag of one nation above that of another nation in time of peace.

U.S. Code, Title 4, Chapter 1, Section 7(g)

IN OTHER WORDS

When flags of more than one nation are displayed, they should be displayed at equal heights on separate staffs. This rule seems a bit confusing, since the flag of no nation should be displayed in a position equal to that of the United States, right (page 90)? Remember, though, that while the flags of all countries should be at the same height, the flag of the United States should be in the *prominent* position. If placing the flags on a stage, for example, the flagstaffs should be at equal heights, but the American flag should be on its own right (and appear to the far left when viewed from the audience, see page 55).

FOR EXAMPLE

At diplomatic meetings, it is customary to display the flags of all of the nations involved. All of the flags are of the same general size and displayed at the same height, but the host nation's flag is placed in the position of honor.

Raising the flag of one nation above another is a symbol of victory in time of war. Lowering the flag of another nation is a diplomatic insult—a veritable declaration of war. For this reason, displaying the flags of multiple nations on separate flagstaffs and at equal prominence is the only option, as either of the other options is a grave insult and an invitation to a good, old-fashioned brawl. This is why the United States flag takes a position of prominence (that is, its position, not its height) but is not raised above the flags of other nations. As all students of international protocol and diplomacy know, it is never a good idea to insult anyone's country, flag, or mother.

DID YOU KNOW?

In its early years, the United States made payments to the Barbary States, including Tripoli. The pasha of Tripoli felt that United States' payments were insufficient, and as a sign of his displeasure he ordered the flagstaff in front of the United States consulate to be chopped down. In response to this symbolic insult, existing tensions in the region escalated and the United States responded as though it had been attacked in an act of war. American Stephen Decatur took possession of a fortress owned by Tripoli. The American flag was raised over the fort, a symbol of American victory, and this war became the first time that an American flag was flown in victory on the soil of an old-world country.

Using Staffs When Flying the American Flag with the Flag of Your State, Locality, or Society

THE CODE

THE FLAG OF THE UNITED STATES OF AMERICA should be at the center and at the highest point of the group when a number of flags of States or localities or pennants of societies are grouped and displayed from staffs.

U.S. Code, Title 4, Chapter 1, Section 7(e)

THE FLAG OF THE UNITED STATES OF AMERICA, when it is displayed with another flag against a wall from crossed staffs, should be on the right, the flag's own right, and its staff should be in front of the staff of the other flag.

U.S. Code, Title 4, Chapter 1, Section 7(d)

IN OTHER WORDS

The writers of the code were very careful to exactly specify all the ways that the American flag can and should be displayed in the position of honor. This honor extends all the way to the staff of the flag itself, which is always in the position of honor in front of another flag's staff.

Although this may seem to be commonsense material, there are a few gray areas. What about raising and lowering the flags? Some state flag codes, including those of the states of Vermont and Texas, require that when the flag of the state and the flag of the United States are displayed on adjacent staffs, the flag of the United States should be raised first and lowered last. This sign of respect should be followed in every state of the Union, regardless of what local law provides, because it is also required by our national flag code.

ALSO

> WHEN THE FLAGS ARE FLOWN FROM ADJACENT STAFFS, the flag of the United States should be hoisted first and lowered last.
>
> *U.S. Code, Title 4, Chapter 1, Section 7(f)*

WHY IS THIS?
It's all about honoring the flag, even when the rules don't quite make sense. After all, the American flag's staff must be on the outside, above the other staffs. At the same time, it must be placed on the wall first. Therefore, the other flag must be slid under the American staff, then slid out again at the end of the ceremony.

DID YOU KNOW?
Some people believe that the Texas state flag may be displayed in the center or above the American flag. This opinion is based on the fact that the Republic of Texas entered the Union via a treaty, and was at one point its own country. Despite this, the American flag should still be hoisted first and placed in a position of prominence next to the Texas state flag.

Flying the American Flag on the Same Halyard as the Flag of Your State, Locality, or Society

IN OTHER WORDS

It's fine to fly the flag of a "lower level" political entity or organization on the same halyard (rope) as an American flag, as long as it's lower down the line. Remember that the flag of another nation should not be displayed on the same halyard as that of the American flag.

FOR EXAMPLE

When flying your American flag and state flag together, it is proper to raise the American flag first and fly it at the peak of the pole. Many states specify in their state flag codes that the American flag is to fly above the state flag, with the flags of municipalities below.

ALSO

> ADVERTISING SIGNS should not be fastened to a staff or halyard from which the flag is flown.
>
> *U.S. Code, Title 4, Chapter 1, Section 8(i)*

WHY IS THIS?

Flags of states, cities, and municipalities are lower-level, more local divisions of our governmental system. They too are representative of the will of the people, and are therefore worthy of flying on the same cord as the American flag. The same is true of societies and organizations. They don't represent the public, but their intentions are civic-minded and noncommercial. It is not acceptable, however, to fly the flag of a business on the same cord as the flag. Why? Because the person flying the commercial flag ostensibly wants people to notice the American flag (and adjacent commercial flag) because of a desire to sell more products.

DID YOU KNOW?

Although not specifically the flag of any society or organization, the MIA/POW flag may be flown directly beneath the flag of the United States on the same halyard. In fact, the MIA/POW flag may be flown above a state flag, unless state law requires otherwise. The MIA/POW flag was developed in 1971 at the suggestion of the wife of a missing U.S. soldier to commemorate prisoners of war and those missing in action during the Vietnam War. Congress has designated the MIA/POW flag (in PL 101-355) as "the symbol of our Nation's concern and commitment to resolving as fully as possible the fates of Americans still prisoner, missing and unaccounted for in Southeast Asia, thus ending the uncertainty for their families and the Nation." Other than Old Glory, the MIA/POW flag is the only flag ever to have flown over the White House.

Flying the Union Down

THE CODE

THE FLAG SHOULD NEVER BE DISPLAYED WITH THE UNION DOWN, except as a signal of dire distress in instances of extreme danger to life or property.

U.S. Code, Title 4, Chapter 1, Section 8(a)

IN OTHER WORDS

Flying your flag upside down is a serious breach of etiquette. So serious, in fact, that you would do it only as a signal that your life or property is in danger. Thus, flying the flag this way has become the perfect way to signal for help in a life-threatening situation.

FOR EXAMPLE

How serious is flying a flag upside down? During the 1992 World Series between the Atlanta Braves and the Toronto Blue Jays, a group of U.S. Marines found out the hard way when they flew the Canadian flag upside down. This action offended many Canadians, but in the end they had the last laugh. Their flag may have been flown upside down, but they were not in distress. Toronto ended up winning that year's World Series in six games.

WHY IS THIS?

The use of the upside-down flag as a distress signal arises from a maritime custom predating radio communication. The upside-down flag alerted others that a boat was in distress, and served as a call for help.

In 2003, an Alamosa, Colorado, businessman flew the American flag upside down in his store window as a protest against the war in Iraq. He had read in an old Boy Scout manual that flying the flag upside down is a sign of distress, and he felt that the war was a sign that the *entire country* was in a dire state of distress. Alamosa's chief of police disagreed and threatened to prosecute the man under an old Colorado law that holds that "contempt of flag" is a crime. To avoid prosecution, the man removed the flag but contacted the American Civil Liberties Union. The town eventually settled with the businessman and allowed him to fly his flag as he pleased. Other protesters have used the flag in this manner as well, and many have been threatened, both legally and with the baseball bats of other angry citizens. Whether the protesters are desecrating the flag or exercising their right to free speech remains a matter of debate.

Carrying the Flag

IN OTHER WORDS

When displaying the flag as you walk (as opposed to carrying a folded flag), the code specifies how your flag must be carried. You can't just have four people carrying a flag, one on each corner, and you can't just wad it up and sling it over your shoulder. It's got to *fly*, even if you're walking only a few hundred feet. If you're going any distance at all, or spending any time carrying the flag, you should use a flagstaff. It is acceptable either to hold the staff tilting in front of you, away from the body, or to rest the staff on your right shoulder, allowing the flag to fly freely above and behind your head. Your flag should never touch the ground.

FOR EXAMPLE

A military color guard consists of military personnel who carry the flag on a flagstaff as part of their duties. Being a member of the color guard is a great honor for the bearers and an inspiring sight for viewers. The Marine Corps color guard, for instance, carries Old Glory (flag's own right, of course, see page 50) and the Battle Color, which is decorated with fifty streamers commemorating the military campaigns in which the marines have participated. They do not carry the flag flat. The members of the color guard display the colors during a two-year tour at parades, ceremonies, and functions throughout the United States and abroad.

WHY IS THIS?

If your flag is carried horizontally or vertically, it is not visible to onlookers. There is also some speculation that the flag should not be carried horizontally or vertically because of the association with carrying a flag on a casket during a funeral service. Most important, though, this is another example of how the flag must always be allowed to fly aloft and free, a symbol of the freedom and strength we hold dear.

DID YOU KNOW?

Most people carrying the flag have a couple of miles to walk at most. If they think that their arms are tired, they should speak to Elle Milner. Ms. Milner, a single mother of two from Portland, Oregon, walked 4,500 miles carrying an American flag donated by Portland Fire Station No. 25 to the city of New York. Several fire departments along her route volunteered to carry the flag through their towns, and she was greeted by ten New York City firefighters and police officers when she arrived at the end of the journey on Memorial Day, more than five months after it began. Ms. Milner's goal was to bring the country together following the tragic events of September 11; she called her journey the "Patriot Line."

Storing the Flag

Proper storage can prolong the life of your flag, so make note of these important rules and suggestions:

- Your flag must be completely dry before you store it. Dampness can cause folds to create permanent creases in your flag. Moreover, mold and mildew grow on damp fabric, so it is ideal to place your flag in a moisture-proof bag.
- If your flag is permanently affixed to a staff, it should be carefully furled, wrapped in a case or in plastic, and stored upright.
- If your flag is not on a staff, the best fold is the triangular fold with the union out (see page 82). There are numerous special triangular storage units for flags, from inexpensive zip-up plastic bags to beautiful wood and metal display boxes.
- The place where you store your flag should be well ventilated. Your flag should not be placed near harsh chemicals or cleaners.
- Be sure to keep your flagpole or staff in good repair. Rust can cause a flag to rip, its fabric to be eaten away, or create permanent stains.

It is acceptable to clean or repair a flag as long as the overall condition of the flag is serviceable, and the dimensions of the flag are not altered by the repairs. In fact, cleaning your flag regularly can prolong its life, since some dirt can damage the fabric. An outdoor flag may be hand-washed with mild detergent. Many dry cleaners offer free flag cleaning, especially during the month of July. Flags may be patched with iron-on patches, but never repair a flag if the repair will be overtly noticeable.

Soiled or Unclean Flags

IN OTHER WORDS

There is a common misconception that any flag that touches the ground must be burned. The flag, in fact, must be destroyed only when it is no longer a fitting emblem. A small, repairable rip or a bit of dirt that can be cleaned are not reasons to destroy a flag; stains, fraying, or larger tears are. The most dignified way to dispose of a flag is in a burning ceremony.

FOR EXAMPLE

Organizations such as the Boy Scouts of America or the Veterans of Foreign Wars often plan flag-burning ceremonies on Memorial Day, Flag Day, and other times. Such ceremonies begin with the Pledge of Allegiance and may include the playing or singing of a patriotic song before the flag is ignited, stripes first, away from the union. These ceremonies are usually free and open to the general public.

WHY IS THIS?

If burning seems a barbarous way to dispose of the flag, think of the alternatives: throwing the flag into the garbage to be ground up and tossed into a dump pile, or burying it under the ground and allowing it to molder. Burning has always been a sign of purification and rebirth, and the flame destroys the flag in a dignified manner without allowing it to become more soiled or worn. Nobody knows exactly when the first flag was burned, but the practice was popularized by civic and patriotic groups early in the twentieth century.

DID YOU KNOW?

It is ironic that the most dignified and legal way of disposing of a flag is also the method used by those protesting the flag and government-related activities. Although many states and municipalities have anti-flag desecration statues on their books, in 1989 the U.S. Supreme Court ruled that such laws are unconstitutional violations of free speech. The Supreme Court held that burning the flag was a form of expression comparable to speech, and was thus protected by the First Amendment. Justice William Brennan wrote: "We can imagine no more appropriate response to burning a flag than waving one's own, no better way to counter a flag burner's message than by saluting the flag that burns . . . We do not consecrate the flag by punishing its desecration, for in doing so we dilute the freedom that this cherished emblem represents." Many Americans disagree with the Supreme Court ruling and feel that burning the flag in protest goes beyond negative expression and is an attack on America, and that waving the flag alone is not sufficient to counteract the perceived desecration of the burning of the flag. There have been efforts by some legislators to add a flag-burning amendment to the U.S. Constitution, eliminating First Amendment protection for flag burners. At the time of this writing, the debate continues.

PART FOUR

The Abuse of the American Flag

Endangering the Flag

IN OTHER WORDS

Use common sense when displaying or storing your flag. Anything that could tear, soil, or damage a flag should be avoided. A flag might look good on top of a house, but if the flag is downwind from your chimney, you risk soot or, even worse, *sparks*. Placing a flag beachfront in high winds risks tearing. Placing a flag atop a pile of old paint and kerosene is just asking for trouble.

FOR EXAMPLE

Although it might seem patriotic to buy American flag mud flaps, placing them on a car is sure to damage the image of the flag.

WHY IS THIS?

The flag is a symbol of a living country and is itself considered a living thing. Would you neglect and damage a living thing?

DID YOU KNOW?

In honor of America's bicentennial in 1976, an enormous flag, the largest in the world at the time, was constructed by famed flag manufacturer Annin & Company. The flag measured 199 by 360 feet—approximately the size of a football field. The flag was hung from the Verrazano-Narrows Bridge as part of the Operation Sail festivities, a ceremony in which thousands of boats, decked with American flags, sailed through the New York harbor. Unfortunately, the flag was not manufactured to withstand the strong winds over the bridge. It lasted a grand total of two hours before becoming damaged beyond repair.

Draping the Flag

THE CODE

THE FLAG SHOULD NEVER TOUCH ANYTHING BENEATH IT, such as the ground, the floor, water, or merchandise.

U.S. Code, Title 4, Chapter 1, Section 8(b)

IN OTHER WORDS

How many times has it been said that the flag must fly free? If it is draped over a banister, a branch, or a display of soda cans, it is not flying free. If your flag does not fit in the space you envision for it, you can either move it, knock down a wall or railing, or finally get rid of that pile of old magazines you're never going to read anyway. When the flag is displayed in a store, this violation is especially egregious. Draping a flag over merchandise not only hinders the freedom of the flag, it looks suspiciously like a utilization of the flag for the purpose of advertising something unrelated to our federal government (see page 115).

Allowing the flag to touch the ground is a sign of disrespect, and it can generate some powerful emotions in Americans. In 1996, the Phoenix Art Museum held an exhibit entitled *Old Glory: The American Flag in Contemporary Art*. Among the pieces in the exhibit was a work by Kate Millet called *The American Dream Goes to Pot*, in which an American flag was stuffed into a toilet. Another piece, entitled *What is the Proper Way to Display a U.S. Flag?*, by artist Dread Scott, featured an American flag lying on the ground. The director and curator of the museum felt that the artists were exercising their First Amendment rights. Protesters, including many U.S. veterans, felt differently. They stormed the building, removing the flag from the toilet and hanging the flag that was on the ground up on a wall. The flags were later replaced in the works.

ALSO

THE FLAG SHOULD NEVER BE used as a covering for a ceiling.

U.S. Code, Title 4, Chapter 1, Section 8(f)

WHY IS THIS?

Because the code requires that the flag fly freely, displaying it in such a way that it cannot fly is a violation. A flag cannot fly freely when it's stapled to the ceiling, and it also cannot fly freely if it's on the floor. Give your flag some space.

DID YOU KNOW?

The flag should never be draped on the ground, but the code says nothing about a flag that is *grown* from the ground. In Lompoc, California, a flower field grows in the dimensions and design of the American flag. The field spans 6.65 acres and consists of more than two million flowers. The fifty stars alone are the result of planting roughly 400,000 white larkspur flowers. The flag is clearly visible from the air, though from the ground it appears to be just another beautiful field of flowers.

Decorating with the Flag

THE CODE

[THE FLAG] SHOULD NEVER BE festooned, drawn back, nor up, in folds, but always allowed to fall free. Bunting of blue, white, and red, always arranged with the blue above, the white in the middle, and the red below, should be used for covering a speaker's desk, draping the front of the platform, and for decoration in general.

U.S. Code, Title 4, Chapter 1, Section 8(d)

IN OTHER WORDS

The flag should not be used for decoration. It should appear behind a speaker, not as a tassel to hang off the stage. It should never be used as a curtain. The proper way to create a patriotic background or display is simply to use a combination of red, white, and blue materials. Bunting is a fabric type specifically designed with these colors for use as decoration. It usually comes in a "patriotic rainbow" and should be hung with blue on top, white in the middle, and red below.

FOR EXAMPLE

Red, white, and blue bunting has been around since the creation of the flag and is most commonly associated with political conventions, which are prone to be swathed in thousands of yards of bunting and many red, white, and blue balloons. Bunting usage has become increasingly popular; it was even a key design element in Macy's department store 2001 holiday window display in New York City, with red, white, and blue bunting displayed at the top of each window. Not a traditional Christmas decoration, perhaps, but patriotism knows no season.

WHY IS THIS?

When drawn up or gathered into folds, the American flag becomes a mere decorative element and not the symbol of our country. The American flag can be an item of decor, but only when allowed to be itself: the living symbol of the United States. Even the very *image* of the American flag should not be used as decoration. Stars and stripes are both appropriate, but only if they are used in a way that evokes the American flag without mimicking it.

Red, white, and blue bunting is the proper way to use the flag's colors in decoration.

Using a flag as decorative bunting has, in at least one case, played a part in American history. When President Lincoln visited Ford's Theatre on April 14, 1865, his box seats were draped with bunched flags, which was common at the time. John Wilkes Booth crept up and shot Lincoln from behind, then jumped onto the railing and yelled *"Sic semper tyrannis"* ("Thus always to tyrants"). He then planned to leap down to the stage and make his escape. However, as he leapt, his spur caught on the decorative flag, which was bunched at the railing, causing him to lose his balance, land awkwardly, and injure his leg. He did escape but was captured nearby a few days later.

For many years, it was popularly held that the flag that had reached up and grabbed the villain was none other than Old Glory herself, but it turns out that the actual hero was the flag of the Treasury Department Regimental Unit.

The Flag and Abraham Lincoln

Like many other important figures in American history, Abraham Lincoln's life and legacy are associated with the American flag. While George Washington has been falsely credited with creating or inspiring the design of the flag, it was during the presidency of Lincoln—those turbulent years of the Civil War—that the flag became the beloved emblem it remains today.

The Civil War was a war symbolized by a flag. The southern states no longer wanted the Stars and Stripes; they wanted their own flag, known as the Stars and Bars. (The Stars and Bars flag had several variations, much like other early flags.) The attack on Fort Sumter in April 1861 that started the war would leave two dead, and would end when the American flag was fired upon and lowered to the Palmetto flag of South Carolina. This insult to the American flag, and by extension to the Union, created a fervent allegiance to the Stars and Stripes, and soon flags were waving proudly from schoolhouses, churches, and houses across the northern states. After the start of the war, in fact, American flags became so popular that makers couldn't keep up

Stars and Bars flag, 7-star version

Stars and Bars flag, 13-star version

with the demand. In New York, the orders were so numerous, and the shortage of material so severe, that the price of flag bunting rose from $4.75 to $28 per yard. Book muslin, used for the stars, increased in price almost 30,000 percent.

Which brings us to President Lincoln, whose presidency had been intertwined with the flag since his first inauguration. On the way to that inauguration, Lincoln gave an impromptu speech in Philadelphia in which he said he'd rather be assassinated than surrender the flag. Eerie—especially since political assassination was very uncommon in Lincoln's day. In fact, Lincoln was the first United States president to be assassinated.

Then, during Lincoln's inauguration ceremony, the halyard on the flag above the White House broke and the flag was torn in two. Eventually, the damaged flag was wrestled to the ground and a new, unblemished flag flown in its place, an extraordinary metaphor for the Civil War that would define Lincoln's presidency and change the course of American history.

This makes it all the more poignant that Lincoln would reach for the beloved American flag at the moment he was shot. Or so the story goes. It's true that there were flags adorning the presidential box at Ford's Theatre on the night of Lincoln's assassination. It seems unlikely, though—despite eyewitness accounts—that Lincoln would have reached for one of them in his moment of peril, as the president was shot at point-blank range and fell into a coma almost immediately.

A flag was used to cushion Lincoln's head, however, as he was moved from the theater to the home of a tailor named William Petersen. That flag, stained with the dying president's blood, disappeared for several generations before it was donated to a local museum in rural Pike County, Pennsylvania, where it can still be seen today.

Wrapping with the Flag

IN OTHER WORDS

The flag should never be used to wrap or carry anything else. As patriotic as serving your hamburger buns from a flag-lined basket, wrapping a present in a flag, or carrying your clothes hobo-style in a flag might seem, these are not correct uses of the American flag.

FOR EXAMPLE

It is possible to buy products such as American flag wrapping paper and chocolate wrapped in American flag packaging. Such products are, most likely, bought by patriotic Americans, but it doesn't honor the American flag to have this paper wrapped around candy, then thrown out with the trash. Red, white, and blue candies would be a better choice.

WHY IS THIS?

The flag is not a tool. It is not something that is used to help you perform a practical task. Its purpose is to help you remember the honor and glory of your country. Instead, simply consider using red, white, and blue bunting or paper.

Using the flag as wrapping may be more than innocent error or carelessness; it can also make a political statement. In 2003, during the war in Iraq, an unidentified Iranian man, angered over the war, created a hand-painted American flag and used it to wrap his donkey. On the other side of the world, a U.S. citizen wrapped his bulldog in the American flag in support of America's troops. Both men intended to make a statement with the flag, one dishonoring the country, one supporting its troops. Neither was correctly displaying the American flag, but both no doubt had really, really warm animals.

Advertising with the Flag

THE CODE

THE FLAG SHOULD NEVER BE USED FOR ADVERTISING purposes in any manner whatsoever.

U.S. Code, Title 4, Chapter 1, Section 8(i)

IN OTHER WORDS

It doesn't get much more clear than that. Don't use the flag to sell stuff. Ever. That includes waving it behind a product in a television advertisement or wrapping it around a model in a magazine ad. Of course there is an exception. It's perfectly fine to use a picture of the American flag on the package when you're actually selling an American flag.

FOR EXAMPLE

What about the cover of this book? Isn't a book cover an advertisement for that book? The answer is yes, and therefore the flag should never appear on a book cover . . . except when that book is actually about the American flag. A book about improving your marriage or learning to clip your toenails, for example, should never feature the author draped in an American flag. That's a sales gimmick, no matter how patriotic that toenail-clipping expert claims to be.

WHY IS THIS?

There's advertising, and then there's advertising. Accurately telling consumers what your product is (a flag; a book about the flag) is one thing. Associating your product (a doughnut, a tire, a car wash) with the flag merely because it's a powerful symbol that most people have positive feelings about is something entirely different. It's manipulative. It's insulting to the flag. The flag is an important symbol of the United States, not a tool with which to sell beer.

DID YOU KNOW?

The debate over the use of the American flag in advertising is not a new one. In fact, one of the first U.S. Supreme Court cases about a state law involved the use of the flag in beer advertisements. In 1878, Congress debated a law that would criminalize the use of the American flag in advertising. Although there was strong support in Congress against using the flag for commercial purposes, the law did not pass. Commentators have suggested that many congressmen were afraid that if they passed a broad law forbidding the use of the flag in advertising, they would then not be able to use the flag in their own political campaigns.

The Case of the Giant Misused Flag

Although the flag should never be used for advertising, a brief look at a magazine or television would suggest that this part of the code is being flagrantly violated. Flags are used to sell everything from trucks to peanuts. When patriotic fervor is at a high pitch, companies print calendars featuring American flags to give away to their customers. Although inappropriate, flags appear on posters and in music videos. Don't be fooled; this is just a more subtle form of advertising.

Where is the line drawn between correct usage and an advertisement? The answer is in the *intent*. If the flag is intended to make a political or social statement, that is acceptable. If the flag is intended to get your attention or invoke feelings of patriotism so that you will think more highly of the company, that is unacceptable. The problem is this: how do you know what the true intent is?

As an example, let's take some of the most egregious abusers of the flag as advertisement: gas stations and car dealerships. These businesses often fly giant flags. What's the problem? *Intent.*

In the 1960s and '70s, many cities instituted laws limiting the height and number of signs a business can have on its grounds. But these laws don't apply to American flags, which aren't technically advertising signs. Sales of flags started to skyrocket as many businesses—and especially gas stations and car dealerships—began to use American flags as visual attractants for their customers.

The practice of advertising with the flag continues. Today, it's not uncommon to see flags that make Mary Pickersgill's enormous Star-Spangled Banner look like a handkerchief!

Writing on the Flag

IN OTHER WORDS

Nothing should be added to or placed upon the flag. A flag should not be written or drawn upon. No decals, insignias, or other designs should be sewn, drawn, or otherwise placed upon the flag.

FOR EXAMPLE

Many celebrities recognize that it is disrespectful to write on the American flag. A fan handed golfer Jack Nicklaus an American flag to sign after he had played in the Bay Hill Invitational. "You don't sign an American flag," Mr. Nicklaus was reported as saying, handing back the flag. "That's not what you do."

WHY IS THIS?

The flag is complete as it is. It does not require additions, no matter how small or well intentioned. Any drawings or other additions to the flag desecrate it as a complete and living symbol of the United States.

There is an exception made to this rule in the case of important events, such as memorials for victims of tragedy or war. The Smithsonian's National Museum of American History owns one such flag that is a powerful symbol for all Americans, especially African Americans. The 84th Regiment U.S. Colored Infantry fought on the side of the Union during the American Civil War. The regiment carried its colors into battle and printed on the flag's stripes the names and dates of the campaigns the men fought in Texas and Louisiana. The flag was not merely memorabilia for these battles (that would be a violation of the spirit of the code) but a rallying point for the troops, reminding them of the freedom they were fighting for and the people they were liberating in the name of the United States. Every battle written on that flag symbolized one step closer to freedom, and one step forward for all mankind.

Advertising and Mutilation of the Flag, Criminal Penalties

ANY PERSON WHO, within the District of Columbia, in any manner, for exhibition or display, shall place or cause to be placed any word, figure, mark, picture, design, drawing, or any advertisement of any nature upon any flag . . . of the United States of America; or shall expose or cause to be exposed to public view any such flag upon which will have been printed, painted, or otherwise placed . . . any advertisement of any nature; or who, within the District of Columbia, shall manufacture, sell, expose to sale, or to public view, or give away or have in possession for sale, or to be given away for use for any purpose . . . an article of merchandise . . . or a receptacle for merchandise or article or thing for carrying or transporting merchandise, upon which shall be printed, painted, attached, or otherwise placed a representation of any such flag . . . shall be deemed guilty of a misdemeanor and shall be punished by a fine not exceeding $100 or imprisonment for not more than thirty days, or both, in the discretion of the court.

U.S. Code, Title 4, Chapter 1, Section 3

IN OTHER WORDS

In Washington, D.C., and only in Washington, D.C., our capital, it is illegal to write on or affix anything to a flag. It is illegal to expose a flag that contains an advertisement to public view. It is illegal to sell, give away, or possess for sale any merchandise that contains a representation of a flag.

FOR EXAMPLE

Selling a T-shirt with an American flag and the slogan "these colors don't run" on a street corner near the White House can theoretically land a person in jail for up to thirty days. In fact, since the definition of "flag" is very broad—a couple of stars and a few stripes on a printed flyer would be a flag under this definition (see below)—theoretically, Congressman Trent Lott could be arrested for autographing a picture with just a corner of the flag showing; Bruce Springsteen could be arrested for autographing his album *Born in the U.S.A.*; the president could be arrested for signing his official Oval Office photograph. The list goes on and on.

ALSO

THE WORDS "FLAG, STANDARD, COLORS, OR ENSIGN," as used herein, shall include any . . . picture or representation of [the flag] . . . made of any substance or represented on any substance, of any size . . . upon which shall be shown the colors, the stars and stripes, in any number of either thereof, or of any part or parts of either, by which the average person seeing the same without deliberation may believe the same to represent the flag, colors, standard, or ensign of the United States of America.

U.S. Code, Title 4, Chapter 1, Section 3

WHY IS THIS?

The District of Columbia is an odd legal entity, for it is not as independent as a state but is also not indistinguishable from the federal government. The District of Columbia does have a degree of self-rule, but it is still controlled by the federal government. That means it is the only area where Congress is free to impose special fines and criminal penalties for desecration of the flag. So Congress did.

DID YOU KNOW?

This law has been widely criticized as, at the least, overly broad and, at the worst, unconstitutional. In fact, the law is included in a book on strange laws, entitled, *You May Not Tie an Alligator to a Fire Hydrant: 101 Real Dumb Laws*, by Jeff Koon and Andy Powell (who were high school students when they wrote the book). The law is listed alongside the prohibition against training a bear to wrestle in Alabama and the law against takeout hamburgers on Sunday in Oklahoma. Whether or not the flag law is on the same level as prohibiting the tying of an alligator to a fire hydrant is a matter of debate, but what is clear is that the law is largely ignored in Washington, D.C. Many Americans not only fail to think buying an American flag T-shirt between visits to the Washington Monument and the Smithsonian Institution is a crime, they consider doing so a patriotic act. That's probably why you can't throw a rock in the capital without hitting someone peddling flag-related trinkets. (It's also, by the way, illegal to hit people with rocks in Washington, D.C.)

Printed and Embroidered Flags

THE CODE

[THE FLAG] SHOULD NOT BE EMBROIDERED on such articles as cushions or handkerchiefs and the like, printed or otherwise impressed on paper napkins or boxes or anything that is designed for temporary use and discard.

U.S. Code, Title 4, Chapter 1, Section 8(i)

IN OTHER WORDS

Go into your kitchen and throw out those patriotic paper plates. Get rid of those Fourth of July paper picnic cups. And if you have an American flag handkerchief, shame on you.

FOR EXAMPLE

In spite of this prohibition in the code, disposable products imprinted with the American flag are widely available. American flag napkins, plates, candles, fans, hats, noisemakers, and pencils are available from a wide variety of distributors. Gag stores and Web sites also feature American flag litter boxes and toilets!

WHY IS THIS?

The reason for this prohibition is simple: the American flag should not be sat upon, dirtied, or thrown away. The American flag, as a symbol of the country, is not disposable like other objects. If printing or writing on the American flag is unpatriotic, how much less patriotic is it to wipe barbeque sauce from your fingers or blow your nose on the image of the symbol of our country?

DID YOU KNOW?

Although most people buy products such as American flag napkins and plates with the intention of being patriotic, not all people who use such products are doing so out of simple love of country. During the 1960s, many antiwar activists felt that the American flag had become a symbol of aggression and imperialism rather than of freedom. Abbie Hoffman, a founder of the Yippies, used an American flag handkerchief. Although Mr. Hoffman sometimes used the American flag as a positive symbol—he sported an American flag shirt at congressional hearings to show that he considered himself a true patriot—the use of the flag handkerchief can only be seen as a symbol of protest. Most people who buy American flag napkins aren't doing so to protest anything, so they might want to consider the symbolism of their actions the next time they host a cookout.

The Flag on Clothing and Bedding

IN OTHER WORDS

The American flag simply should not appear on household items or your clothing, especially a bikini or your underwear. The flag should not be part of the design of a uniform, but a patch may be added to the uniforms of soldiers, firemen, policemen, and members of civic organizations. A Boy Scout may wear a patch on his uniform, but a burger flipper should not.

FOR EXAMPLE

Some American designers and retailers have marketed a variety of American flag-inspired items, from American flag T-shirts to glittery rhinestone-encrusted flag sweaters. Believe it or not, according to the code, these items are unpatriotic!

WHY IS THIS?

For the first two hundred years of our country's history, it was almost unheard of to wear clothing that featured the American flag. This all began to change in the 1960s, when wearing a flag became a symbol of protest for many Americans, and a symbol of patriotism for others. Flag clothing really took off around the time of the bicentennial in 1976, when everything from pantyhose to fire hydrants got a red, white, and blue facelift. Today, wearing the flag is so common that it has become acceptable to almost every American. The statute on the previous page is basically ignored, and for the most part rightly so, as a relic of the past. Not so sure that it should be relegated to the dustbin of history? Consider the following.

Shortly after September 11, 2001, many sports teams added flag patches to their uniforms. Technically, the teams should not have done so, but in this case the gesture was clearly patriotic and supportive of the United States in a time of crisis.

One prominent opponent of this rage for flag-wear is Stan Tiner. At a U.S. Senate hearing on the possibility of a flag-desecration Constitutional Amendment, Mr. Tiner, a Vietnam veteran and former editor of the *Mobile Register* in Alabama, claimed that ordinary, well-meaning citizens often desecrate the flag as badly as protesters. "What of those who have taken the flag for commercial purposes and emblazoned its image on everything from hats to luggage to swimsuits and underwear?" he said. "Are those blatant acts of profiteering on the image of the flag appropriate or respectful of our flag?" Apparently, to the many Americans who continue to buy such products, the answer to that question is "yes."

DID YOU KNOW?

Although many acts of wearing the flag are seen as patriotic, some are meant to be a challenge to the status quo. Larry Flynt, controversial publisher of *Hustler* magazine, wore the American flag as a diaper at a court appearance. Gross, offensive, and unpatriotic, right? Now, stop and consider the fact that a national retail chain recently sold very similar patriotic diapers. The "Little Patriots" diapers, as they were called, were covered in red, white, and blue stars. The packaging showed a baby sitting in front of a large American flag—a clear violation of the prohibition against using the flag for purposes of advertising.

The Right Way to Wear the Flag

THE CODE

THE FLAG REPRESENTS a living country and is itself considered a living thing. Therefore, the lapel pin being a replica, should be worn on the left lapel near the heart.

U.S. Code, Title 4, Chapter 1, Section 8(j)

IN OTHER WORDS

There is one right way to wear the flag. A flag lapel pin can be worn securely on the left side, near the heart, the center of life in your body.

FOR EXAMPLE

American government leaders are often seen wearing American flag lapel pins. Prominent television journalist Bill Moyers, feeling that such pins were being worn exclusively by conservative politicians, wore one on the PBS program *Now*. Mr. Moyers said that he wanted to reclaim the flag for more liberal Americans because it had been "hijacked and turned into a logo—the trademark of a monopoly on patriotism." Flag replicas are worn throughout the country as a symbol of patriotism by individuals at either end of the political spectrum.

WHY IS THIS?

Because the flag is treated as a living thing, if it is to be worn, it should be on the left side where the heart beats.

In the aftermath of September 11, 2001, *ABC News* asked its staff members not to wear American flag lapel pins, red, white, and blue ribbons, or any other patriotic symbols. ABC wanted its on-air personalities to maintain an image of neutrality. ABC spokesman Jeffrey Schneider said: "We cannot signal through outward symbols how we feel, even if the cause is justified. Overseas, it could be perceived that we're just mouthpieces for the U.S. government, and that can place our journalists in danger." This move was met with much criticism in the news community and elsewhere. Many feel that patriotic symbols do not jeopardize neutrality but instead show support for one's fellow Americans.

Afterword

A PERSON GETS FROM A SYMBOL the meaning he puts into it.

United States Supreme Court, 1943

If there is one theme in this book, it is this: cherish the flag as the physical embodiment of the glory of our words and deeds and never take it for granted. Most Americans have seen thousands of flags in their lifetimes—in our neighborhoods, our gas stations, and our laser-light shows—so it is easy to lose that sense of wonder. The problem is not with the flag, however; it is with us. No matter what our attitude, the flag does mean something. When the flag was shot off the mast of Stephen Decatur's boat during a firefight with the British in 1812, a sailor jumped overboard *during the heat of the battle* in order to save it. Why? Because the flag meant something. Because it may have been the only American flag he had ever seen. Because he was in awe of the freedom and opportunity this new country of America intended to give all its citizens.

You can put that kind of meaning back into the American flag by not letting it fly untended for days at a time; by not letting it hang loose and tattered from your car antenna; by refusing to wear it on your clothing or to use it as a mere decoration for your backyard summer barbecue. Serving a greasy burger on an American flag paper plate or wearing your American flag T-shirt to mow the grass is a worse violation of that flag than never looking at the flag at all. Scoff if you will, but the fact remains that officially our national flag code considers it more dangerous to our country for citizens to wipe their ketchup-stained fingers on an American flag napkin than to burn the flag in protest over our government's policies.

Is it old-fashioned to love the flag? Is it square to know the rules and follow them? Is it curmudgeonly to point out the common, everyday abuses of well-intentioned Americans? Perhaps, but consider these inspiring words from George Soper, printed in the April 20, 1917 edition of the *New York Times*:

> *How are we to excuse the abuse of the flag which we see every day? . . . [The flag] is widely used for advertising purposes, being draped about signs announcing auctions, bargain sales, lofts to let, so-called automobile opportunities, shoes, corsets, candles, cameras, imitation jewelry, gum, lager beer, fishing tackle and many other things not ordinarily associated with patriotic sentiment. Show windows are draped and festooned with colors with no other apparent object than to make shrewd business use of the responsive feelings which are thus aroused. . . . Is this patriotic?*
>
> *There are those that would question whether it is patriotic to carelessly hang Old Glory from the window ledges, often wrong side out, and leave it there untended . . . until the winds have nearly swept it away or wound it into a tangle. . . .*
>
> *Do not hang the flag from a window ledge or balcony. If you must hang it down the side of your building, do not let it hang there too long. Never crowd it into a space too small for it, or display it from your motor car. . . .*
>
> *Do not display the national flag in front of your house except on patriotic occasions. It means something to your neighbors to see you bring it out; the sight quickens the blood and rouses within every American an inward, if not audible, cheer. It means little that is credible to its owner to see the flag day after day neglected, bedraggled, begrimed, and virtually forgotten. . . . Preserve and protect your flag as you would preserve the noble sentiment which it represents.*

Further Reading

The best source of information about the American flag is the United States government. The full text of the United States Code, including the fifteen pages dealing with the national flag, is available at www.access.gpo.gov. Other statutes, amendments, and orders can be found at the National Archive in Washington, D.C., or on the Internet at www.archives.gov. In 1989, the House of Representatives published a book called *Our Flag*, which is a fine source of facts and figures. All this information is available to the public, and we encourage you to learn more about our government and its laws.

For a well-written, entertaining look at the history of the American flag, we highly recommend *For Which It Stands: An Anecdotal History of the American Flag* by Michael Corcoran (Simon & Schuster, 2002). The works of George Henry Preble and W. W. Wannamaker are excellent references on the American flag for the more historically inclined and are available in your local library or bookstore. If they are not, request that they be ordered.

United We Stand (Chronicle, 2001) and *Long May She Wave* (Ten Speed Press, 2001) are beautiful photo works on the American flag that show this proud symbol in its best light.

If this book has inspired you to take up a serious study of the American flag, contact the North American Vexillological Association (NAVA). Vexillology is the study of flags, and these folks can tell you everything you'll ever need to know about the American flag—and any other flag, too. To find out more, visit their Web site at www.nava.org.

Index